THREEFOLD METHOD FOR UNDERSTANDING THE SEVEN RAYS

and

OTHER ESSAYS IN ESOTERIC PSYCHOLOGY

by
Kurt Abraham

LAMPUS PRESS
P. O. Box 541
Cape May, New Jersey 08204

DEDICATED TO
ALL EARNEST STUDENTS
OF THE SEVEN RAYS

BOOKS BY KURT ABRAHAM

Psychological Types and the Seven Rays - Vol. I

Threefold Method for Understanding the Seven Rays and
Other Essays in Esoteric Psychology

CREDITS

CONTENTS

Roll and return, and roll again.
Cycle around the circle of the Heavens.
Prove all is one.
Quality. . . . . the harmony of the spheres.

Esoteric Psychology, vol. I.

A THREEFOLD METHOD FOR UNDERSTANDING THE SEVEN RAY ENERGIES*

How can one acquire knowledge and understanding of the seven rays? Through a threefold method that could be outlined in the following manner:

1. Through an academic, theoretical familiarization with the rays, leading to an attraction to certain rays, and to an approximate and conjectural knowledge of one's own rays. This is primarily the approach of the intellect.

2. Through a concerted effort to recognize and appreciate the rays which are *not* part of one's own ray equipment. This leads to a recognition of the *group interplay* of the seven rays. This approach employs the technique of sacrifice and is indicative of the soul.

3. Through the effort to *become* another ray and eventually all the rays, relatively speaking. This approach is a path of considerable resistance and is indicative of the spiritual will.

There is little that need be said in respect to the first stage, for it is a stage that is generally self-evident to the intelligent investigator. One point could be mentioned, however, and that is the need to guard against an over-intellectualization of the subject matter. D. K. makes an interesting comment related to this in *Esoteric Healing*: "Again, I have to respect how vast is the subject with which we are dealing, and all these earlier instructions and the answers which I give to the questions only serve to show how abstruse the matter is. But if you will have patience and will be willing to learn by absorption more than by analysis, you will later discover that you know much — intuitively and discriminately."[1] He also suggests that in the study of this matter one should "read slowly."[2] The point is, to begin the study we have no choice but to use the intellect, to read, to study, to analyze and to observe ourselves and others. But the intellectual approach ought not to be overemphasized. Why is this so? Because of the nature of the knowledge involved. A ray is defined as "a particular force or type

*See glossary (p. 108) for short definition-description of the seven ray energies.

of energy, with the emphasis upon the quality which that force exhibits and not upon the form aspect which it creates."[3] The intellect is of special value when dealing directly and exclusively with the quantitative and exoteric world of forms, of appearances and of effects. When dealing with the qualitative world of consciousness, of esoteric energies, of relative causes, the intellect, although necessary, plays a less prominant role.

It is clear that the intellect "learns by analysis" but what is it that "learns by absorption"? At one level it is the emotional body, and at another level it is the causal body or soul. Analysis deals more with separation, whereas absorption deals more with an integrating-unifying-synthesizing process. Analysis is more of an intellectually conscious process, whereas absorption is both a subconscious and a super-conscious process. Analysis enables us to bring our present knowledge and understanding to bear on a particular subject. Absorption enables us to "consult", in a sense, recesses of our psyche which are not quickly and readily accessible to the intellectual faculties. There is a wisdom within us that can respond to and sort out and unify matters, when approached with patience, right motive and a certain sensitive inner listening.

There is also an interesting distinction here between analysis and discrimination. To analyze is to separate, to take apart. To discriminate is to determine the value of something, not to place it side by side as in analysis but to place it in a sort of hierarchical order. Analysis deals more specifically with the quantitative world of forms. Discrimination deals more specifically with the world of quality and consciousness.

Knowledge and understanding of the rays are, therefore, not something that one can acquire quickly through a pressing and concentrated intellectual approach. Rather slow and careful reading, gradual absorption and assimilation, leading to reflective discrimination and the intuition, are the keynotes of the process.

The Group Interplay of Ray Energies

The first stage has brought us to an academic familiarization with the rays and a gradual absorption of the knowledge into the deeper recesses of our psyche or soul. During this process there generally is a very strong tendency to be attracted to certain rays and to repel others, to like some and to dislike others. On the positive side, this will often give us clues as to our own ray type. On the negative side, one could say that this is merely a continuation of the personality consciousness which tends to prevent a recognition of the group interplay of ray energies. One could take advantage of the positive factor, however, to acquire some deeper knowledge and understanding of one or two rays. This in turn may enable us in some degree to enter more deeply into the esoteric world of energies.

Some obstacles to Recognizing the Group Interplay of Ray Energies. How are we to come to a recognition of the group interplay of ray energies? How are we to recognize and to understand a type of energy unlike our own? Carl Jung wrote: "It is my conviction that a basis for the settlement of conflicting views would be found in the recognition of different types of attitude — a recognition not only of the existence of such types, but also of the fact that every man is so imprisoned in his type that he is simply incapable of fully understanding another standpoint."[4] In the process of recognizing the group interplay of energies, it is perhaps first of all necessary to recognize what a difficult process this is. We are so "imprisoned" in our own type that it becomes extremely difficult to recognize, let alone understand, other types. In a certain sense, then, it becomes necessary to *recognize what we do not know*, not so much in a form sense (though that might provide a clue) but in a qualitative sense. When we recognize more clearly what we do not know, then we open ourselves consciously to the complementary contribution of other parts, facilitating then a group interplay of energies.

There are certain tendencies that the personal or "I" consciousness has that prevent a clear and open recognition of "the other" or that which one does not know. First of all, there is the tendency *to fear* what one does not know, resulting in a defensive fleeing or a defensive attacking. Secondly, there is a tendency *to ignore* what one does not know, hence, ignorance. Thirdly, there is the tendency *to pretend* that one knows. Fourthly, there is the tendency *to belittle* or demean what one does not know. As Carl Jung wrote: "If one does not understand a person, one tends to regard him as a fool."[5] An opposite of this and our fifth point is the tendency to disproportionately *exalt* what one does know. Perhaps this is similar to what Jung called the "demon of self-admiration." A sixth tendency is *to project* what we do know — our own type — onto situations that we know little about, resulting in inaccuracies and distortions. These six tendencies — fearing the other, ignoring the other, pretending that we are the other, belittling the other, exalting the self, and projecting the self onto the other — all militate against a recognition of the special complementary contribution of the group interplay of ray energies.

Determining the Ray of the Situation-Problem. There is an attitude and a technique that can aid in the elimination of the distortions of the personal perspective and help us see the group nature of things. The attitude is that of the *detached observer*. The technique is that of *determining the ray needs of the situation-problem itself*. In cultivating the attitude of the detached observer, it is necessary to recall again and again that we are endeavoring to make observations in esoteric realms, employing the esoteric sense. That is to say that the visible and objective worlds are vehicles for invisible, subjective, casual factors. We are moving from a recognition of form to a recognition of quality, from characteristic to archetypal pattern, from event to psychological and spiritual law. To observe in a detached fashion is to observe our own reactions in such a way that the personal pain-pleasure principle is not a predominating factor. In other words, a psychologically painful event (embarrassing, humiliating, risky, evocative of criticism, discomforting, detrimental to reputation, offensive to self-esteem, etc.) may be especially instructive. As a small child acquaints himself with the laws of the physical plane through painful bumps and bruises, so also do we acquaint ourselves with psychological laws through emotional, mental and personality abrasions and mini-crises. Beyond the personal pain of it, the abrasions become lessons and, therefore, blessings. Consciousness has been quickened, new awareness and new recognitions are the result, which are priceless joys. There is a *design* to the abrasions and conflicts. There is a *hidden symbol* contained therein. There is an *esoteric meaning* to it all. There is a special opportunity within the obstacle. But if one is not detached, if one is personally involved, the design and meaning elude one. The abrasions then serve only to slow one down rather than serve as catalysts of transmutation.

A situation or problem is generally of such a nature that it can best be approached or resolved through a particular type of qualitative energy or combination of qualitative energies. (Examples will be given below in the effort to elucidate this point.) The tendency, however, is to *project* one's own energy type onto a particular situation-problem and, if possible, to *impose* one's own energy type onto a particular situation-problem, in spite of the fact that it may be qualitatively inappropriate.

Darwin — Imposing Fifth Ray Method on a Fourth Ray Situation. In the book *Psychological Types and the Seven Rays*, vol. I. I drew attention to Charles Darwin's unique method of "verse-making" as reported in his autobiography. His school assignment was to write a poem — something that Darwin found exceptionally difficult. "I had many friends," he wrote, "and got together a grand collection of old verses, which by patching together, sometimes aided by other boys, I could work into any subject."[6] What sort of qualified energy is required in order to write poetry? What is the energy of the situation-problem itself? The writing of poetry is a *creative* process. Unlike the scientific investigator who is trying to observe what is already there, the poet is trying to create a new form. The poet is also concerned with *self-expression*. The "self" in this sense is an inner, perhaps, spiritual or psychological state. The expression generally and traditionally concerns itself with a sense of *beauty*. If we look at the pure or pronounced type, the scientific investigator is not at all concerned with any of these basic elements or qualified energies. The scientist examines the form; the poet creates a new form. The poet expresses himself; the scientist detaches himself to observe what is. The poet is profoundly concerned with beauty; the scientist considers beauty as more or less irrelevant. Darwin's response to the essentially fourth ray situation-problem, was to *impose* his own predominantly fifth ray energy onto the situation. He gathered a "grand collection" of old verses much in the manner of gathering a grand collection of beetles, which was one of his first scientific projects. Instead of creating new forms, he "patched together" various existing forms. Instead of meeting the situation-problem with the appropriate energy and immersing himself in that energy, he circumvented the situation. Although he completed the assignment, in actuality avoided the true work of it. Strangely enough, it was apparently easier for him to go to some length to gather existing works, than it was for him to sit down and think in a creative and artistic mode. For those conditioned by the forth ray, the opposite would tend to be true. The creative approach would tend to be much easier than an extensive research approach.

What would be a more appropriate way to deal with the situation-problem if one wanted to approach the group interplay of ray energies? With a theoretical knowledge of the rays one could attempt to assess the situation in terms of most appropriate energy. Secondly, one could gauge one's own attraction or repulsion, one's own relative facility or ignorance vis-a-vis the energy requirements of the situation. Thirdly, if there was a lack of facility and there was a repulsion (fear, ignorance, belittling, etc.) in regard to the situation-problem, then one could make some attempt to engage oneself in the activity in some little but significant way. As part of this step it is particularly beneficial to associate oneself with those who are already somewhat adept at using the energy. One could then observe the appropriate energy very closely and in action.

This is a very simple example since we are dealing with a young person and a pronounced type. As well as the fourth ray, other rays can also be of special use in the creative process, such as the second, the third and the seventh rays. Both the fourth ray and the fifth ray could condition a person, which would tend to result in an ability to deal appropriately with situation-problems of both domains, relatively speaking.

First Ray Situation of a Job Interview. The following situation-problem deals with a nurse being interviewed for a job in a nursing home. In her words:

> The first question the directress asked me was where I went to school. This was puzzling to me since that information was on the application. She fired one question after another at me about my education and experience. Many questions verged on personal matters. This got me upset because I started opening up to her and I hadn't prepared an answer for this type of question. She really delved into personal matters. I responded as if she where an understanding person, but she wasn't. When I started to explain myself there was no indication that she had even heard me. What really upset me was the repetition of one question after another with no real response or indication to me that she was really listening to the answer. The impression that I got was that she really wanted to see how I would handle a stressful situation. She was testing me to see how I would respond, not caring what I actually said. The *manner* in which I responded was apparently more important. I was emotionally on the verge of crying. I felt somewhat violated by her energy.

What knowledge can the seven rays shed on this particular situation? The situation itself as interview is primarily a first ray situation. In the hiring of a person we are dealing with an important administrative decision that is related to the "preparing of the form." The job itself, however, is not a job-situation in which the first ray energy is of great importance, although individuals with first ray in their equipment could be capable of handling such a job and in certain circumstances could be capable of making a special contribution. There is a certain amount of scientific knowledge necessary in order to perform nursing duties, which suggests the fifth ray. The seventh ray can also be of particular value in the practical application of scientific knowledge. Nursing is also one of the healing arts and, therefore, the second and seventh rays are of special value here. With the interview situation the first ray plays a major role. With the nursing situation rays two, five and seven play special roles.

The interviewee, the nurse, was thinking more of the job itself than of the interview situation. Through my analysis of this individual, it seems to me that there are three rays of some development and prominence in her psychological equipment: There is the second ray at the soul level, the third ray conditioning the personality, and the fifth ray conditioning the mind. Also present are a sixth ray emotional body and a third ray physical. She is conscious to a degree of the qualities that she has and the appropriateness of these qualities to her chosen profession. The situation of the interview was, therefore, very confusing to her, since it did not seem to address these very important qualities.

The interviewer, the administrator, was necessarily in the position of control and dominance during the interview. She very likely has a first ray mind as many (though certainly not all) administrators do. She was apparently exercising much power and control over the interviewee. She fired questions at the nurse more in the style of an interrogator than an interviewer. She asked several personal questions, overstepping conventional limits of the situation and, thus, subtly abusing her power. What her motives were for this we do not know. Perhaps the nurse was partially right in her suspicion that the administrator was really testing her to see how she "would handle a stressful situation." Perhaps the administrator was trying to make some sort of impression of power through the negatives of fear and intimidation. Perhaps the administrator was trying to hide something of herself behind the disconcerting attack on another, thereby concealing the true motive, as it were.

The nurse's confusion occurred partly as a result of projecting the "bubble" or the "colored sphere" of her own psychological ray equipment onto a situation-problem which is not ruled by the type of energy she was utilizing. To do anything else would have been exceptionally difficult. Familiarity with the rays, however, and the types of situations governed by the various rays could have mitigated the confusion and at least reduced her vulnerability in the situation.

The nurse was quite right in recognizing her own contribution to the service work in which she was engaged. She had acquired and was continuing to acquire scientific, academic (fifth ray) knowledge in her profession. She was also familiarizing herself with healing techniques that are still innovatively beyond the present scope of established academic community, so one could say that her interests and contribution went far beyond the normal routine of duty. Less visible, yet present, is her love and dedication to the service work of healing, which is one of several factors suggesting a second ray soul. The nurse, then, entered the situation of the interview with an attitude, a psychological sphere, a qualitative world, highly conditioned by the fifth and second ray energies. The interviewer and the situation of the interview itself are both of the first ray type, a type of energy not in the equipment of the person being interviewed. The situation was further confounded by the inappropriately aggressive use of the first ray energy, which tends to intimidate and generate either fear and submission or hatred and rebellion.

The question is, then, what would be the best way for such a person as the nurse to conduct herself energy-wise in such a situation? First of all one would have to recognize that this is "foreign" territory for her, and, as such, it is a little frightening or at least discomforting. The situation *according to ray type* is not familiar to her. Secondly, one would have to recognize that one's own ray equipment ought not to be unduly projected if inappropriate to the immediate situation, which once again can be somewhat disconcerting. How can one deal, for example, with a scientific situation-problem if one does not employ the scientific attitude and energy? And how, as in Darwin's case, can one deal with a purely creative fourth ray situation if one does not employ fourth ray energy (although two, three and seven can also be of value in the creative situation)? And how in this case can one deal with first ray power situations if one does not understand to some degree the subtleties of power? The answer is: one will deal with it *naively, foolishly, disruptively* or deal with it *not at all*. The way that our nurse friend dealt with the situation was naively. The naive person can be taken advantage of — which she was. She was also, however, offered the job. But she did not take it, for she did not care to work under such a supervisor — which resulted then in her not wanting to deal with the situation at all.

We find here then an abrasive and disruptive force emanation coming from the administrator. The administrator was playing some sort of power game. Unfamiliar with first ray matters and with the use or misuse of power, there are several *lessons* that one could *extract* from the situation, if one managed to achieve some degree of detached observation. Our nurse friend managed to make the observation that the administrator was possibly *testing her to see how she would handle a stressful situation*. Emotional control. Self-control. Poise under fire. Control over oneself leads to control over situations that involve others. How can responsibility be delegated to those who are not in control of themselves?

One could then scan one's past experience to determine whether or not we are dealing with an isolated situation or if the situation in any way is related to a general principle or law. In my own experience I have observed that a new employee is often given a task that is especially difficult to perform. He is given the task without warning, as if it were merely a routine task. His employers or immediate superiors pretend that the task is so routine that they themselves are paying very little attention to it. They are, however, surreptitiously observing him very very closely. They are, in fact, *testing* him. The initial tests are peripheral. That is, even though there is some degree of difficulty, the tasks are peripheral enough to the organization that they cannot cause the organization itself any real harm. The organization is "insulated", as it were, from the possible mistakes a neophyte could make. Perhaps the administrator who was testing the nurse preferred the initial testing in her own office, where a patient's life was not of concern.

In the book *Psychic Discoveries Behind the Iron Curtain* there is an interesting account of how Stalin tested the psychic Wolf Messing. As the authors put it: "Stalin commanded a straight-forward, horrendous trial of Messing's talent. He was to pull off a psychic bank robbery and get 100,000 rubles from the Moscow Gosbank where he was unknown." After doing this, he was given "a more intriguing task from a dictator's point of view. Messing was taken to an important government office — perhaps inside the

Kremlin. Three different sets of security guards were ordered not to let Messing leave the room or the building. He had no exit pass. 'I fulfilled the assignment without difficulty,' says Messing, 'but when I stepped outside into the street I couldn't resist turning and waving at the high government official watching from the top floor window of the room I just left.' "[7] It is interesting to note that Stalin did not call in a group of scientific thinkers to scrutinize Messing, rather he put him through some exceptionally difficult tests that from one angle could be called "real life" situations.

Tentatively, we might be on the track of something peculiarly first ray. Traditionally, the academic type of testing and the scientific type of testing deal with the theoretical situation or the situation in which an isolated variable is being scrutinized. Apparently, there may be a first ray type of testing that forces one to integrate all components — past experience, theoretical concepts, basic intelligence, self-control, alertness, intuitive ability, etc.—bringing them to a point of *dynamic synthesis*. The effort is to determine not what the person says he is, not what he theoretically conceptualizes, not what he does in the artificial situation — but what he *is*. In other words the factor of *being* is what is being tested.

The specific factor that was being tested by the administrator could possibly have been self-control and more specifically emotional control. From our theoretical study we "know" that emotional control is of particular importance to the first ray type. "First ray people dread emotion and despise it."[8] Emotion can cloud thought. It can interfer with that all important presence-of-mind and skill-in-action. Could the administrator have been firing questions at the nurse in the effort to disrupt her, that is, test her emotional equanimity? Or was the administrator simply endeavoring to firmly establish her own position of power through the technique of instilling fear? Was the administrator primarily concerned that others fearfully, quickly and obediently carry out her directives? Many of the human situations in which we have the opportunity to view the rays are situations where the dominant tone is one of personality distortion. Precisely here is it difficult to achieve detachment, to observe impersonally, and to recognize and appreciate the quality of the ray as an archetype rather than as an unpleasant human characteristic.

Another lesson to learn from this incident is the need for protection, the need not to feel or be "violated by her energy." Power necessarily protects itself. Power does not place itself in a vulnerable position. There were two factors which opened our nurse friend to violation. First of all she got "upset." If you get upset, you lose your "centering", and your emotions play havoc with your thoughts and consequently with your speech. Secondly, she made the mistake of "opening up to her", of "explaining myself", of answering questions "on personal matters." In opening up in this way one is revealing sensitive areas, soft points, or delicate matters. A person can misuse this shared knowledge, which becomes then a form of betrayal. On the other hand, being able to share one's heart-felt thoughts with the right person greatly strenghtens one. It is, therefore, a delicate matter which ought not to be done easily or casually. In the situation of an interview that deals with the power (first ray) factor of hiring or not hiring, the interviewer knows that he or she has a right to certain information regarding the interviewee. This information deals primarily with the applicant's past educational and job experience. Strictly speaking, that's all that the interviewee need reveal. The interviewer, however, generally wants more information — information of a personal nature. This he may obtain through other people — much hiring is done through personal recommendations from people whom one knows and whose opinion one values and trusts. Or the interviewer may probe personal areas during the interview, usually in a delicate manner. The first ray type instinctually knows how to be *impersonal*, that is, pleasant, polite but not too personal. They know how to assume a point of isolated strength. Other types, particularly the two-four-six types, do not achieve a right impersonality with ease. They also do not readily determine the impersonal question from the subtly personal one. A clever interviewer may slip in an apparently innocouus personal question between several impersonal ones. Or the interviewer may exercise his power by implying that although this is a personal question, you must still answer it if you expect to be considered for the job. But even a subtly personal question a first ray type is quick to identify and can even pretend to answer in a personal way, while evading issues that are too personal. On the other hand, a person responding to a two-four-six type of energy may tend to reveal too much too quickly and, thereby, lose one's protective center of power.

The objective is to come to recognize and appreciate to some degree the rays "foreign" to us or unlike our own in order that we might come to recognize and appreciate the group interplay of ray energies. The attitude of the detached observer and a technique of determining the ray needs of the situation-problem itself are needed in order to prevent the projection of our own rays indiscriminately onto all situations. In the case of Darwin's verse-making the tendency was to project or impose his own method (fifth ray) onto a fourth (or second or seventh) ray situation. The opportunity to observe something of the qualitative energy of a ray life was thereby lost. In the case of the nurse being interviewed, the effort was to project a warm second ray and a knowledgeable fifth ray note onto a situation-problem that required a first ray poise, control, impersonality and first ray recognition of the power factor. In Darwin's case the impostition was cleverly and personally successful in that it accomplished his goal of meeting the academic requirements as painlessly as possible. From a soul point of view, however, it was not successful in that the opportunity to take a step towards wholeness was evaded. In the case of the nurse being interviewed, the imposition was personally unsuccessful. The administrator held firm, did not bend, and the interviewee was "violated." The situation, however, from a soul point of view had some success to it, for greater self-awareness was stimulated and some reflective thought as to the qualitative life of a "foreign" ray was initiated. In spite of the unpleasantness of the situation itself, there were identifiable first ray factors that provide some food for reflective thought. Among these were: the technique of testing in such a way that all available faculties are synthesized, the testing for poise and emotional control, a period of testing prior to delegating responsiblity, and the need for a protective impersonality or an ability to "insulate" oneself from the abrasive forces of others.

A Combined Military, First Ray, and Scientific, Fifth Ray, Situation-Problem.

Vannevar Bush — engineer, inventor, administrator — combined in some way rays one and five, and he was, therefore, able to move intelligently within the domain of these two energies, relative to the human predicament. Those he met were not always capable of doing so. In describing a particular admiral in the U.S. Navy during the Second World War, Bush wrote:

> It was well known that he [Admiral King] scared his junior officers so thoroughly that often he didn't get adequate information through them. Characteristically, our discussion opened as follows: King scowled and said, "I have agreed to meet you, but this is a military question, and it must be decided

on a military basis, to which you can hardly contribute." So I told him, "It is a combined military and technical question, and on the latter you are a babe in arms and not entitled to an opinion." It was a good start, and the discussion went on from there — and went well.[9]

During the First World War, Vannevar Bush had been working on the invention of a submarine detection device. He discovered towards the end of the war that there were several other groups working on similar devices:

The point is that their scheme was a lot simpler than the gadget I was developing. It was not as good in some ways, because my device signalled by the cessation of the tone when the seeking ship was immediately over the submarine and theirs gave the signal later, but their device was simple, was cheap to build, and could have been put into use in quantities in a hurry . . . . I think if I had known about that system and known that there were nonpolarizing electrodes that would have worked that way, as I did not, I probably would have seen how the two ideas could have been combined. The reason they were not was that there was no centralizing group able to bring together parallel efforts and compare them.[10]

Initially then we find the fifth ray of scientific knowledge working in its somewhat characteristically isolated fashion. Bush had received a doctorate in engineering and, as a young man, turned his scientific skills towards military needs. This brought him into relationship with the domain of the first ray, necessitating in some degree a group interplay of ray energies. Had he been a "pure" fifth ray type, he most likely would have devoted his energies to pure scientific research and probably would not have bothered with the administrative issues of developing "a centralizing group able to bring together parallel efforts and compare them." The more pronounced fifth ray type tends to pursue precision of knowledge for its own sake and often leaves the work of application and correlation to others. Bush, on the other hand, combined both the first and fifth rays, and developed into an able administrator within fifth ray or first and fifth ray fields. He became Dean of Engineering at M.I.T., Vice-President of M.I.T., President of the Carnegie Institute of Washington, and Director of the Office of Scientific

Research and Development during World War II. The latter position of O.S.R.D. enabled him to correct the mistakes he experienced during the First World War, for this was a "centralizing group" that correlated scientific research relating to the military. It also brought the decision making in respect to new weapons to a panel of both scientific and military experts. Earlier the military had made all the decisions, and many of them were poor decisions due to the scientific incompetence of the military personel.

For the sake of survival the group interplay of energies was necessitated. The two types, the two rays, did come together and did cooperate. This cooperation did not come about, however, without struggle and conflict. Both types were specialized in their individual fields. *Only the necessity of the situation, which was both a first and fifth ray situation-problem, brought the two types together in cooperative effort.* Also, those individuals who were conditioned by both rays and, therefore, had access to both rays, were key facilitators in the group interplay of these ray energies. There was no conscious recognition and knowledge of the rays as such, but nevertheless there was a recognition of the type factor. Knowledge of the seven rays could have greatly facilitated the process.

Admiral King approached the matter from a first ray point of view, and here one of the major questions is the responsibility of power. Apparently, one of his techniques in the use of power was to instill fear in his subordinates and also to punctuate the superior position, as he did — or as he tried to do — to Vannevar Bush. ("I have agreed to meet you, but this is a military question, and it must be decided on a military basis, to which you can hardly contribute.") Bush had the perfect repartee, stating that it was a *combined* military and technical question, which put them on equal footing. If Bush was ignorant on military questions, King was equally ignorant on the scientific question. The sense of equality of contribution and mutual respect for one another's contribution is indicative of the recognition of the *fact* of the group interplay of energies. King apparently did come to recognize the power of knowledge (science), as well as first ray power. He was able to recognize in some degree the factor of greater power in the group interplay of energies, in contrast to the impostion of the dictatorial style and personal power.

To use power in such a way as to generate fear and "thoroughly scare" others might win the sensation of personal power for the hour, but it will lose the power for the day or the larger picture, the group picture. Admiral King was not getting "adequate information" through his subordinates because of the fear factor, which affected in a detrimental way his ability to rule or to administrate. (The technique of fear was similarly used by the directress of nursing by whom our friend was interviewed.) On this element of fear Bush made the interesting comment:

> The ways in which management has changed have been many, but predominantly it has become more human. This alteration has been due to many things. The organization of labor, facile transportation, wider knowledge of affairs, have rendered nearly obsolete the old management through fear which could function all too successfully when a whole town's very life depended on the nod of a factory owner.[11]

The recognition of group interplay requires the opposite of fear, which is love, trust, respect, the ability to identify the good qualities of others, and the attitude of humbly opening one's mind to the qualitative worlds that one does not know.

Bush summarized his efforts to relate and coordinate the scientific and military point of view in the following way:

> [I]t was not long before civilians and military officers began to understand one another. The officers found that "scientists" could bring together subtle physics and chemistry, but could also do it in an exceedingly practical and hard-boiled manner. The "scientists" found that the officers had something which was new to them and admirable — utter loyalty, the ability to operate smoothly in a rigid system, and the art of command. This tendency toward mutual understanding and respect was greatly furthered by a few individuals.[12]

The fifth ray quality indicated is the ability to "bring together subtle physics and chemistry." The first ray qualities indicated are: "exceedingly practical and hard-boiled", "utter loyalty", the "ability to operate smoothly in a rigid system" and the "art of command." But the main point is that each of the two basic types was recognizing in some degree the qualitative world of the other type. More particularly, the fifth ray types were admiring certain first ray qualities, were adapting to them and probably were becoming in some small degree like them. The first ray types, generally speaking, probably did not enter as deeply into the world of science as the fifth ray types entered the world of government-military. Both were highly developed and specialized in their respective fields but utter beginners ("babes in arms") in the "foreign" field.

The 'tendency towards mutual understanding and respect was greatly facilitated by a few individuals." It is reasonable to assume that those "few individuals" embodied in a developed degree elements of both the first and fifth rays. Certainly one of those individuals and perhaps the most prominant among them was Vannevar Bush himself. Bush had the task of not only opening up the military minds to the world of science, but also opening up scientific minds to the fact that the worlds of politics and the military are worlds of extensive and precise knowledge, albeit of a different order.

> Our unique system of government could not operate
> if it were not for the politically able. Let me go a step
> further. It could not operate if it were not for the fact
> that there are sufficient numbers of men who have
> a good grasp of the problems we face as a nation, and
> have also political skill and the ambition to exercise
> it. It is altogether too seldom that we pay tribute to
> such men. But I do believe we come far nearer to a
> proper evaluation than was the case a generation ago.
> I even believe that there are now scientists among
> us who realize that to become a successful politician
> requires as much intellectual prowess, although of a
> far different kind, as it takes to become a successful
> scientist.[13]

Instead of the military mind not adequately appreciating the scientific mind's ability to deal with military matters, we have the scientific mind not adequately recognizing the "intellectual prowess" of the successful politician. And for what reasons? The tendency would be to look at the worst characteristics of the worst politicians, generalizing from there and mistaking that part for the whole. The tendency would also be to look at the best qualities of one's own type and to remark how the politicians do not achieve those standards. Without any knowledge of the seven rays, Bush was recognizing the subtle factor of type and the need to "properly evaluate" and "pay tribute to" the type we tend not to recognize. He had experienced the closed mindedness and the relative ignorance (ignoring) of each type. He had also experienced the great knowledge and abilities of each type. He had experienced how both types need each other. And he labored to integrate these two types. A major part of his life dealt with the group interplay of these two energies. It was the situation-problem that necessitated first a recognition of the "foreign" type and then a cooperative interplay between the types. Bush labored to bring about a *conscious recognition* of this group interplay. He labored to make others *aware of what they did not know,* that they might peak through a "crack in the egg" of a qualitative world outside of — though, paradoxically, inextricably interwoven with — their own qualitative world.

Esoteric Meaning of "Group." When we use the phrase "the group interplay of energies", the term "group" is used as a technical term and in an esoteric sense. *Ex*oterically the word is defined as "two or more figures forming a complete unit in composition"; "a number of individuals could be assembled together around a common interest and would *not* necessarily constitute a *group* in the esoteric sense of the word. In a certain sense we have the following correspondences:

individual	group
personality	soul
part	whole
self-centered	self-forgetfulness, de-centralized
exclusive	inclusive
polarization	polar union

From a *physical* point of view there can be a group in the sense of an assemblage of individuals. From a consciousness point of view, however, among assembled individuals there may not be any true *group* sense at all.

The word "cooperation" comes close to the esoteric sense of group but is not quite synonomous with it. People can cooperate and work together around very selfish interests. The group in the esoteric sense always takes in and includes the larger whole. Therefore, a person working outwardly, that is, physically, relatively alone could still be working in the true group sense. And on the other hand, a person working in the company of others — but in a very self-centered and personal way — may not be functioning in the true group sense at all. Consciousness of the larger whole always takes into inclusive and patient consideration the unit with which the personal unit tends to polarize. For example, an individual working side by side in a personal, competitive way with another individual tends to be conscious of the best characteristics of himself and the inadequacies of the other person. This tends to lead to confrontation and a lack of *group* work, which is that work which transcends the sum of the parts. The larger whole in this case would be the other person. Group work would require a concerted effort to understand and appreciate the qualitative life of the other person that *we do not know*.

Similarly, a business acting in a purely selfish manner and, therefore, disregarding, say, certain ecological factors, would not be acting in a true group sense, although many people would outwardly be assembled around common interests. Where national leaders are always trying to procure their own selfish interests, the true group sense or consciousness of the larger whole (inclusive of other nations) would be lacking. Where a generation exploits its natural resources to the detriment of succeeding generations, similarly the true group sense of the larger whole, which in this case is posterity, would be lacking. The pattern is quite clear: In the personal-selfish-part sense the effort is to procure some advantage for that separated self, which brings an immediate gain but an eventual loss. In the true group sense there is initially a sacrifice (loss), which brings about the manifestation of the greater life or the whole. So, paradoxically, gain becomes loss and loss becomes gain.

Everything then, regardless of how we are assembled or united as a physical constituency, can be regarded in a personal or group sense. In the particular incident of Darwin assembling fragments of poems instead of creating a poem, we find a personal reaction and a failure to reach the more difficult group sense. In the case of the nurse being interviewed we find a lack of the group sense on the part of both parties during the interview. After the interview the nurse gave effort to understand rather than reject the polar point of view. In the case of Vannevar Bush we find a good group sense with its long and patient effort to sacrifice a sense of self and to bring about the "magic" of polar union. (The Second Law of Soul or Group Life is the Law of Magnetic Impulse, also called the Law of Polar Union. See *Esoteric Psychology*, II, p. 109.)

Example of the "Arrivers" and the "Derailed" Executives. There is an interesting article in *Psychology Today* ("What Makes a Top Executive?" by Morgan W. McCall Jr. and Michael M. Lombardo, Feb. 1983) in which highly successful corporate executives ("arrivers") are compared with other executives who tumbled from positions of considerable success (the "derailed"). One who arrived is described as "an intelligent guy with a delightful twinkle in his eye. He could laugh at himself during the toughest of situations. He was a superb negotiator. He could somehow come out of a labor dispute or a dispute among managers with an agreement everyone could live with. I think he did this by getting all around a problem so it didn't get blown. People knew far in advance if something might go wrong. He was too easy on subordinates and peers at times. Line people wondered whether he was tough enough, and sometimes, why he spent so much time worrying about people. He was thrown into special assignments — negotiations, dealing with the press, fix-it projects. He always found a way to move things off dead center." He ended up senior vice-president.

In contrast a derailed executive is described as follows: "He got results but was awfully insensitive about it. Although he could be charming when he wanted to be, he was mostly knees and elbows. He was a superb engineer who came straight up the operations ladder. He had the rare capability of analyzing problems to death, then reconfiguring the pieces into something new. When developing something, he gave subordinates more help than they needed, but once a system was set up, he forgot to mind the store. When things went awry, he usually acted like a bully or stonewalled it, once hiring a difficult employee and turning him over to a subordinate. "It's your problem now," he told him. He rocketed upward through engineering/operations jobs. Once he got high enough, his deficiences caught up with him. He couldn't handle either the scope of his job or the complexity of new ventures. He was a talented guy and not a bad manager, either. I suppose that his over managing, abrasive style never allowed his colleagues to develop and never allowed him to learn from them."

Important energies in the world of business are the third ray (intelligent activity, communication, energy), the first ray (will, purpose, power, administrative and managerial skills) and the seventh ray (organization). In the case of the "derailed" engineer there is suggested the possibility of a highly developed fifth ray factor and the presence of a lesser developed first ray factor. The "superb" engineering ability and the "rare capability of analyzing problems to death" is strongly suggestive of a developed fifth ray energy. The lesser developed first ray energy is suggested by: 'he got results", "mostly knees and elbows", "acted like a bully or stonewalled it", "not a bad manager", and "abrasive style."

He was "not a bad manager." He had some managerial skill. He did not remain in an engineering capacity alone; he rose in the organization, assuming greater administrative responsibilities. But his style was of the abrasive sort, the tough or hard-line approach (all "knees and elbows", "bully"), indicative often of the presence of the first ray of power, though in an unrefined state. The "vices of the ray" given in *Esoteric Psychology* are: "Pride, ambition, willfulness, hardness, arrogance, desire to control others, obstinacy, anger" (vol. I, p. 201). What is evident in the case of the engineer is a highly specialized talent but a lack of wholeness. "Once he got high enough, his deficiences caught up with him." This is a common flaw among developed but over-specialized people. Early achievement along a particular ray energy can bring about a "derailment" if "new" energies are not assimilated and if life's theme of wholeness is not recognized. He undoubtedly had plenty of "signs", but pride can prevent their right interpretation.

In the case of the "arriver" we see first of all that he was "intelligent" and that he had thorough knowledge of the business, for he could "get around a problem" and be a "superb negotiator." He could function in a world dominated by the one-three-seven line of ray energies. There were, however, other special qualities present. He was a "superb negotiator" because he could understand all points of view and come up "with an agreement everyone could live with." There was a tendency to be "too easy on subordinates and peers", not "tough enough", and to spend time "worrying about people." This is strongly suggestive of the presence of a developed second ray and possibly also the presence of the harmonizing qualities of the fourth ray. Into a world dominated by the one-three-seven line, he was able to bring the balancing qualities of the other major line of ray energy, the two-four-six line. Therefore, he was able to operate in a more holistic fashion. He had a true group sense in the esoteric meaning of the word, for he was able to understand the larger picture, the relative whole. The fact that he was able to "laugh at himself during the toughest of situations" and the fact that he could come out of a labor dispute with an agreement that "everyone could live with" suggests a true group sense. To fight for the best possible advantage of one's own group, is no group sense at all.

Out of the study a general rule emerged: "Ability — or inability — to *understand other people's perspectives was the most glaring difference* between the arrivers and the derailed. Only twenty-five percent of the derailed were described as having a special ability with people; among arrivers, the figure was seventy-five percent" (my italics). The derailed engineer had great skill in understanding the technical problem. A person with a one-five or seven-five combination of ray energies could very easily have the tendency to emphasize the scientific, the technical and the administrative-power factors, to the neglect of the more "humanistic" or sensitivity factors. Thus, the form and structure of things could tend to be more important than human beings themselves. A strong second ray influence, on the other hand, could bring about the ability to "understand other people's perspective" and to "worry" or be concerned about people. But to think only of the human factors to the neglect of the technical-organizational problems would be glaringly ludicrious in a business or scientific or governmental setting. Thus a group interplay of energies is what is needed. When we can get an esoteric scientific grasp of these energies, then the whole process will first of all be far less painful, then highly instructive, and then greatly accelerated.

Group Dynamics, Triangles of Energy. In working with groups of people over a period of time certain phenomena generally tend to occur:

1. There is a tendency for a certain ray or combination of rays to dominate the group. Very often it occurs along either the two-four-six line or the one-three-five-seven line.

2. The dominating ray or rays are evidenced through a triangle (or triangles) of individuals. There is generally a key triangle of individuals that provide a sort of power-station of energies — the dominant and controlling note of the group.

3. There is often the tendency for the dominant ray types to exclude the participation of other ray energies. Participation is encouraged as long as the basic note is supported. A "foreign" though vital note is often not recognized or understood as a vitally contributory element.

4. Necessity of the situation-problem itself, requiring a ray energy that is not easily accessible to the dominant note of the group, may force the door open to the needed but "foreign" ray.

5. Access to the unestablished, unmanifested, but needed ray energy can be greatly facilitated if one of the individuals in the key triangle of energies recognizes and understands in some significant degree the quality of and the need for the "foreign" ray energy. If the key triangle of individuals continues to exclude the foreign, complementary ray,

then it is doubtful that crises (opportunities) of expansion will be properly seized. Even the matter of continuing as is (survival) may be brought into question.

Becoming Another Ray

Theme of Wholeness. The theme of wholeness runs throughout the teaching on the seven rays. In the book *Discipleship in the New Age* D.K. suggested to a student: "You would profit much if you studied carefully the rays which are, at this time, lacking in your equipment" (vol. I, pp. 379-80). In the same book he wrote: "It is of value to students to study what rays are *not* represented in the personality equipment. I commend this to your attention..." (vol. I, p. 351). To the disciple L.D.O. (soul ray two, personality ray four, mental ray four, emotional ray two, and physical ray seven) D.K. wrote: "It will be obvious to you that the major line of force in your equipment, relating you to others and facilitating contact, is the second ray with its subsidiary expression, the fourth ray. This is a definite asset and an opportunity but it makes possible certain liabilities. These should be off-set by a stiffening of all first ray tendencies in order to bring about a needed balancing" (vol. I, p. 134). In *Treatise on White Magic* D.K. wrote: "To sum up the situation, it must be noted that the groups in the past have stood for certain aspects of truth and have demonstrated certain ray characteristics. The new group will express all the aspects and have in it members on all the rays" (p. 415). In *The Rays and the Initiations* D.K. stated that "each initiation establishes relationship between the initiate and the ray energy involved, so that gradually (no matter what may be his soul ray or his personality ray) he can work with the quality and the creative aspect of all the rays, though ever retaining a greater facility to work on his own soul ray . . ." (pp. 557-8).

There is the need to determine the rays we *lack*, to develop these rays as a *balancing* factor, and to be able to *work with the quality and the creative aspect of all the rays.*

Martin Buber: Union of Differing Minds. The theme of wholeness runs throughout a variety of philosophical and psychological treatises, and it is expressed in various ways. Martin Buber discussed a "model of the great community" and a "living in unity" in his essay "Education and World-View."

This community is no union of the like-minded, but a geniune living together of men of similar or of complementary natures but of differing minds. Community is the overcoming of *otherness* in living unity.

The question is not one of exercising "tolerance," but of making present the roots of community and its ramafications, of so experiencing and living in the trunk . . . , that one also experiences, as truly as one's own, where and how the *other* boughs branch off and shoot up. It is not a question of a formal apparent understanding on a minimal basis, but of an awareness from the other side of the other's real relation to the truth. What is called for is not "neutrality" but solidarity, a living answering for one another — and mutuality, living reciprocity; not effacing the boundaries between the groups, circles, and parties, but communal recognition of the common reality and communial testing of the common responsibility.[14]

Martin Buber is presenting a polarity here between two elements for the purpose of clarification and quickening insight:

union of like-minded	union of differing minds
sameness	overcoming otherness
tolerance	experiencing the other
formal, minimal understanding	awareness of other
neutrality	solidarity
effacing boundaries	communal recognition of common reality

What are these two poles? The first pole, that of tolerance and neutrality, is not a bad thing and, in fact, is a right goal for a great many people. Buber, however, is taking us a step further. He is taking us into the realm of the higher self or soul. The stage of being attracted to "sameness" and extending a "formal minimal understanding" to the other is indicative of personality development. There is a sort of intellectual recognition that boundaries (form) must be effaced, but the inner accord is missing. The next stage of "awareness of other" is comparable to the stage of recognizing the "group interplay of ray energies" and is indicative of soul. Substituting the word soul (or true group) for community, we could say that soul deals with the "overcoming of otherness in living unity." Experiencing the other "as truly as one's own" is a level of consciousness that is not achieved by the personality caught in the illusion of separateness. To experience the other as truly as one's own and to recognize the group interplay of energies is to bring about a "polar union." This is not a personality tolerance of the other, but an awareness of the other's "real relation to the truth."

Abraham Maslow: Merging as a Part in a Larger Whole. Abraham Maslow discussed a similar issue using different words and from a psychological discipline:

> The achievement of self-actualization (in the sense of autonomy) paradoxically makes *more* possible the transcendence of self, and of self-consciousness and of selfishness. It makes it *easier* for the person to be homonous, i.e., to merge himself as a part in a larger whole than himself.[15]

On the one hand we have the stage of "self-actualization", which grows out of self-consciousness and selfishness, while on the other hand we have a merging with a "larger whole than himself." The point made here is that self-actualization (personality intergration) is necessary as a preliminary step to self-transcendence (soul, the experiencing of the larger whole). According to Maslow:

> The more we understand the whole of Being, the more we can tolerate the simultaneous existence and perception of inconsistencies, of oppositions and of flat contridictions. These seem to be products of partial cognition, and fade away with cognition of the whole.[16]

Indeed, "the more we understand the whole of Being," the more we will be able to come to grips with the inconsistences, oppositions and contradictions apparent in the parts. But how are we to understand the whole of Being? Can this be done scientifically as well as mystically? The teaching on the seven rays (as well as other holistic sciences and teachings) provides us with a great many maps, hypotheses, and clues as to the intrinsic order substanding the outer multiplicity of parts.

Carl Jung: An Unconscious Existing Wholeness. Carl Jung made the following illuminating statement in *Mysterium Coniunctionis*:

> The *causa efficiens et finalis* of this lack of freedom lies in the unconscious and forms that part of the personality which still has to be added to the conscious

man in order to make him whole. At first sight it is but an insignificant fragment — a *lapis exilis, in via eiectus,* and often inconvenient and repellent because it stands for something that demonstrates quite plainly our secret inferiority. This aspect is responsible for our resistance to psychology in general and to the unconscious in particular. But together with this fragment, which could round out our consciousness into a whole, there is in the unconscious an already existing wholeness, the "homo totus" of the Western and the *Chen-yen* (true man) of Chinese alchemy, the round primordial being who represents the greater man within, the Anthropos, who is akin to God. This inner man is of necessity partly unconscious, because consciousness is only part of a man and cannot comprehend the whole. But the whole man is always present, for the fragmentation of the phenomenon "Man" is nothing but an effect of consciousness, which consists only of supraliminal ideas. No psychic content can become conscious unless it possesses a certain energy-charge. If this falls, the content sinks below the threshold and becomes unconscious. The possible contents of consciousness are then sorted out, as the energy-charge separates those capable of becoming conscious from those that are not. The separation gives rise on the one hand to consciousness, whose symbol is the sun, and on the other hand to the shadow, corresponding to the *umbra solis.*[17]

Jung was clarifying the motive factor in consciousness, and he saw on one hand a conscious will and on the other a compulsion, which thwarts our conscious will and our reason. According to Jung, this compulsion deals with an unconscious factor that is urging us towards wholeness. The dichotomy suggested is:

conscious	unconscious
part	whole
resistance to wholeness	existing wholeness
the phenomenon Man	round primordial being
effect of consciousness	greater man within
supraliminal ideas	kinship to God

The dynamics of the condition include the fact that initially the inner compulsion towards wholeness is only an "insignificant fragment." It seems relatively powerless vis-a-vis the "conscious" man or the growing, integrating personality. But gradually, as the personality develops, its weaknesses, or "secret inferiority", or lack of wholeness, becomes more evident. The personality resists and repells the needed change. The greater man within is whole. There is an "already existing wholeness." There ensues then an inner struggle in consciousness between the soul and the personality, between the greater man within and the phenomenon man.

Integration, Unity, Synthesis. One could say that the tendency towards wholeness at the personality level manifests as *integration*. At the soul level it manifests as *unity*. And at the monadic (spiritual will) level it manifests as *synthesis*. In a certain sense, integration deals with the *form*, unity deals with *consciousness* and synthesis deals with *being*. If we consider consciousness at these three levels, one could equate self-consciousness with personality, group-consciousness with soul and God-consciousness with the monad. (There would be some confusion if we compared this analysis with Jung's, since Jung's "unconscious" included superconscious levels and since Jung did not apparently recognize the soul as being "conscious" on its own plane.)

The tendency towards wholeness at the personality level is integration, which deals with form and with intellect. Intellectually one can appreciate the need to work together, to cooperate, to "efface boundaries" and to express at least a "formal apparent understanding on a minimal basis", to use Buber's words. Integration can be thought of internally as the integrating of the three aspects of personality — physical, emotional-sentient, and mental — into a coordinated though self-centered whole. Externally it can be thought of as cooperation among individuals as they form groups, not in the esoteric sense of the word "group" but in the sense of self-serving groups. From a ray point of view, this stage is marked by the development of one's own ray equipment and by the appreciation of similar types.

The tendency towards wholeness at the soul level is unity. Beyond intellectual recognition of wholeness we have here love and understanding of wholeness. It is at this stage that we become aware of the "other's real relation to the truth", again using Buber's words. It is at this stage that "polar union" is experienced, and it is at this stage that the esoteric meaning of "group" becomes clear. Here we recognize that "something" which is "larger" than the individual parts and works through the group as a whole. We recognize "the other" from the "trunk", as it were. That is, we recognize it from the inside or as part of the same life, rather than from the branches with their illusion of separateness. From a ray point of view we experience the group-interplay of ray energies. There is no longer the imposition of the personal will, rather there is the recognition of right relationship in any given situation. Instead of repulsing the "foreign" ray, one marvels at the indispensible play of its qualitative life.

The tendency towards wholeness at the monadic level is synthesis. Beyond the soul stage of loving-that-which-completes-the-whole, at this stage one *is* the whole. As the integrating personality employs the faculty of intellect, and the soul employs the faculty of selfless love, the monad employs the spiritual will. Instead of mistaking our own ray for the whole or imposing our own ray on the whole, as personality is inclined to do, or recognizing and loving the complementary ray, as the soul is able to do, the spiritual will aspect is able in a certain sense *to be* the other ray, to be all the rays, to be the whole.

In the following quote D.K. makes a distinction between Raja Yoga and the coming "Yoga of Synthesis." "Raja Yoga is now receiving emphasis, which is union through the mind. It sounds like a redundancy to speak of union through synthesis, but it is not so. It is union through identification with the whole — not union through realisation or through vision."[18] With realization and vision there is an implied duality. With identification with the whole there is an implied identicalness, oneness or synthesis.

This matter of synthesis, of being the whole, of being another ray, seems far beyond our development, and, therefore, considerations thereof would be for the most part impractical. Yet, perhaps not. Perhaps this matter of synthesis and of being another ray can touch us in some significant way, albeit in an imperfect or "stepped-down mode." The examples given in the remainder of this essay deal with the question: Can a person become another ray type? Can a person blend and fuse with a qualitative energy that is foreign to his own ray equipment? It seems to me that this is a vast and complex question. Therefore, the following examples are merely suggestive of certain principles at work and perhaps also of certain research that could be pursued.

Herbert Kohl: Educator and Social Activist. Initially as an undergraduate Herbert Kohl studied philosophy. Later he became attracted to the field of education and set out to be an elementary school teacher. His first book, *36 Children*, emerged out of this experience. It was a book that was well received and that generated much interested in his innovative teaching principles and methods. At first he concentrated on being a good teacher within the confines of one small classroom. But "quite unexpectedly work in the classroom led me to political and social conflict," as well as to conflict within himself.[19]

As a teacher, Herbert Kohl was outstanding. As an activist for educational-social change and as a person dealing with administrative problems, he had much to learn. In the latter areas there were certain ray deficiences.

During his first year of teaching at a school in Harlem, he "naively opposed the principal . . . at a faculty meeting. Everyone in the room looked shocked, but no one said a word to me." A few months later he was transferred to another school. This in turn shocked him since the principal had earlier indicated that Kohl would remain at the school. The principal in fact "denied knowing anything about the transfer." A teacher more experienced in administrative ways clarified to Kohl that "problems were always dealt with indirectly, leaving the individual bewildered and with no recourse." This was the "nature of the institution" and one had to get used to it if one expected to survive.[20]

One of Herbert Kohl's complaints was that "conflict was never expressed openly on the staff, and people who hated one another lived an uncomfortable truce for years without revealing feelings . . . We were expected to act like professionals and not like people."[21] He also became "obsessed" with such problems as "the lack of books, the repulsive lunches served, the hatred and failure most of the students experienced every day, and the sheer overwhelming misery of daily life at the school . . . I had to do something about everything even if no other adult cared. In despair at having complied with such cruelty for so long, with no knowledge of politics or strategy, and with no sense of how I would act under pressure, I decided to go to people in the community and try to force the principal out. I had no program or plan for change and my main impulse was to destroy, but I wasn't even prepared to do that effectively."[22]

First of all we see a man here who has a profound interest in education, in teaching, in the art of conveying knowledge. We have such characteristics of a first rate teacher as befriending and deeply caring about the students, dealing with curriculum in a creative way so as to generate interest and avoid the deadliness of boredom, and having a keen sensitivity to the psychological condition of the students. While some teachers were only concerned with physical order in the classroom, Herbert Kohl was concerned about the need for positive self-image and positive relationships (emotional order) in order for the learning process to occur. Initially, we find such factors as teaching ability, a deep love or caring, a creative approach, a tendency to enter into conflict in order to achieve harmony, and a sensitivity to the emotional-psychological condition as suggestive of rays two and four or the two-four-six line of ray energies. We also see a naivete vis-a-vis the administrative power question and the nature of the institution. There is a lack of knowledge of politics and strategy. There is no sense of acting under pressure, no ability to plan for political-social change and no effective means for bringing about needed destruction. This suggests the lack of the first ray energy of power. It is interesting that he placed emphasis on 'revealing feelings" and on acting "like people", that is, with human imperfections, likes and dislikes, etc., and he down-graded acting like a professional. Acting like a professional connotes a poise and emotional control generally more indicative of the one-three-five-seven type.

First Attempts at Confrontation: Afraid to Destroy. What was Herbert Kohl's next step? Revealing his feelings to the principal as he had done earlier, was clearly not the way. He went instead to a group of organized parents — Harlem Parents Committee — who were attempting to bring about better conditions and more meaningful education for Black children. The committee wanted to confront the principal and certain individual teachers. Unexpectedly Kohl began to identify with those he had earlier criticized. He began to see them as "scared people, as warm and funny with their families, as unable to get other jobs." He wanted to deal with the issues but he did not want to cause pain to specific individuals. The committee pointed out to him that "nothing would happen but talk unless there was a direct confrontation." Kohl was also reminded that the children were the ones in pain and that this was the cause of his concern. A meeting was called. As predicted, however, nothing happened but talk, since Kohl did not want to bring forth the necessary documented evidence. As a result, "the principal and teachers remained at school for several years until people from the community without the questionable assistance of soft-hearted liberals like myself forced them out and began to make a decent school for their children. I was afraid to destroy and therefore what needed to be built in the school had to wait." Some years later he saw his mistake. They should have been confronted, given the option to change, and, if refused, they should have been forced out by any possible means. "That doesn't mean I should have wasted energy hating or resenting them, or thought of them as less than human. I could retain my identification and compassion — however, they had to go."[23]

We are witnessing a psychological ray transition here. Initially, when dealing with first ray issues, Herbert Kohl approached the matter through expressing feelings, generating conflict, and without any planned strategy. When others more adept at dealing with first ray matters had little difficulty circumventing such confrontations, Herbert Kohl was forced to look for other methods. His next approach was to consult with an organization that was somewhat aligned with his own point of view. This, clearly, is a basic first ray approach. At the next step, however, he faltered and reverted to a fourth ray energy that was inappropriate for the solving of the first ray problem-situation. In *Esoteric Psychology* (vol. I, p. 206) we find "lack of moral courage", "a hatred of causing pain amounting to moral cowardice", "easily overwhelmed by sorrow or failure" as characteristic of some fourth ray types. The inability to cause sorrow and pain, and the inability to destroy, can result in the perpetuation of sorrowful and painful and destructive situations. But the art of destruction, so necessary to bring about change, is a first ray energy that Kohl was not able to wield. One of the reasons for this is that he identified too much with the emotional matters and he himself got too emotional when wielding a destructive force, in preparation for reconstruction along more spiritual or humane lines. This, however, he was beginning to realize. He was beginning to realize that in the process of wielding a destructive force one does not have to "waste energy hating or resenting." Indeed, one could retain much "compassion." It is interesting, then, that at one point Kohl complained that people who hated one another did not reveal their feelings. And now, after a little more first ray experience, he was saying that one does not have to waste energy hating. One could say that perhaps he himself was becoming more "professional."

Other Ways: The Beginning of Kohl's Own Institution. After the publication and success of his book *36 Children*, he was offered money by the Carnegie Corporation to develop a teacher training program. He formed a group called "Other Ways", became affiliated with the Berkeley Unified School District, and set up shop in a storefront in Berkeley, California.

Other Ways was a small organization-institution. Herbert Kohl was a developed teacher and educational philosopher, but he knew little about running an organization. As a philosopher-thinker, one generates grand ideas, but bringing them into manifestation is quite another matter. Two things he was learning quickly: self-control and taking one small step at a time. He was learning to "use the least possible energy when dealing with the school board or the police." He was also learning "how to keep my anger from corrupting my work." He was realizing that there was a lot of energy available to him and that he contributed to its dissipation through "doing stupid things — yelling, trying to intimidate people, feeling guilty, getting drunk, hating myself." His new method was to "do the modest work and look for openings so that more can develop."[24]

These matters of conserving energy, of being brief, not saying too much, controlling anger, not yelling, not hating or intimidating, etc., and moving along modestly step by step, looking for little openings, are basic and axiomatic to most first ray types. To Herb Kohl, unschooled in the art of first ray matters, they came as a revelation. The reverse of the situation, however, would tend also to be true. That is, many first ray types tend not to be good teachers and may tend to be novices in the philosophical abstractions that come more easily to the two-four type. Herb Kohl, on the one hand, probably became impatiently upset with some administrators and some teachers for their lack of understanding of certain basic, sound and philosophically subtle pedagogic principles. And on the other hand, administrators had to deal with Kohl's lack of knowledge and refinement on the power related administrative questions.

Order and Power Versus Human Values. Kohl felt that "public institutions such as schools, hospitals, or prisons value order and power (over the student or patient or prisoner) above caring humane values."[25] "Order and power" suggest rays seven and one, while "caring humane values" suggest the two-four-six ray influence and especially a ray two influence. Again we see Kohl's emphasis on one of these aspects and a downgrading or belittling of the other. Was Kohl seeing the whole of the situation-problem, the reality of the situation-problem, or was his own somewhat pronounced and unbalanced ray equipment creating a situation where he was keenly aware of some matters and blind to other salient matters? Was there a distortion here due to ray type? As Kohl accused the institutions of being "uncaring," could one not also accuse the warm-hearted and caring ones of not assuming enough responsibility in dealing with the many difficult problems of maintaining a necessary order? Was Herbert Kohl himself not alighting in a particular institution, criticizing it for not meeting his own very high ideals, and then flying off to some other idealistic enterprise before the long labor of change and improvement had even begun? If Kohl had never taken on the administrative responsibilities of an institution himself, this prejudice would likely have continued indefinitely. Assuming certain administrative responsibilities himself, he was forced in some degree to assimilate something of this "foreign" energy.

Uncomfortable in Role of Boss. From a first ray point of view Herbert Kohl's storefront teacher-training center was unorthodox, indeed. Posters and notices were distributed around the schools, announcing Monday afternoon events, such as "happenings, writing sessions, poetry readings," after which everyone "just talked and talked about schools, kids, racism, revolution, hopelessness, hope." He served wine, beer, soda, coffee, potato chips, and pretzels. A lot of kids showed up after school, also about twenty to fifty teachers. The sessions "were fun."[26]

He employed a handful of people to assist him in his project. What sort of structure did he set up? According to him, the group "eliminated the usual cultural roles of boss, expert, secretary, consultant, and found ourselves filling the void with more archetypal forms — elders, fathers, mothers, clowns, priests, jesters."[27] In a way this family structure speaks to the emotional climate and bonding of the group, but it does not speak to the efficiency or to the impersonality needed in an institutional structure. It is interesting that Kohl refers to the boss-expert-secretary roles as 'cultural" and the elders-fathers-mothers-clowns roles as "archetypal." It is interesting because he is in effect minimizing or belittling the boss-secretary, etc., roles as being not as profoundly significant as the "archetypal roles." Boss-expert, etc., are just as archetypal as the other roles mentioned. The boss-kings-rulers-emperors-warriors, etc., had their consultants-experts in the form of wisemen, sages, astrologers, sooth-sayers, doctors, medicine men, etc. In other words, to his "elders, fathers, mothers, clowns, priests, jesters" (note the 2-4-6 emphasis with the latter three), he need only add "kings, princes, dukes, knights, squires," etc., to suggest something of the archetypal roles of the one-seven line. So the differentiation he is making is actually a false one or a distorted one due to ray type. It is also interesting that the very first authority or ruling-responsibility figures one meets are the fathers and the mothers. It seems that with anything beyond that he was very uncomfortable.

As to his own place in this scheme, he said: "The role of father provider and manager was more comfortable to me at the time than that of project director or boss. Externally I was the project director, the responsible party, the highest paid citizen, the accountable one, the boss. I was not comfortable with that role, yet had to embody at least the appearances for the sake of the Berkeley United School District and the Carnegie Corporation of New York. It was easier to take that burden as a family member than as a project director. I did not want the responsibility of being the sole and ultimate source of decisions, since I was floundering as much as anyone else. After all, how do you change this incredibly resilient and resistent culture?"[28]

We have here then a young man who complained and even ranted and raved at times about the state of affairs of educational institutions. He severly criticized those who were in the positions of responsible decision making. When the opportunity presented itself for him to be in such a role, he avoided the responsibility. He was not "comfortable" with the role as boss — and 'comfortable" is a key word here. We are comfortable in circumstances that we understand and at which we perform well. An unfamiliar energy tends to cause discomfort. Initially there is the stage of no discomfort due to non-recognition or ignorance or naivete. Then there is the stage of discomfort due to the recognition that one is in fact dealing with a "foreign" or unfamiliar or potentially antagonistic energy. Once the energy is understood, then there is comfort and ease of activity and relationship. The only way it can be truly understood is when something of the foreign energy becomes assimilated or becomes part of one's own energy equipment. There is a certain resistance to this process, and this is what Herbert Kohl was experiencing in respect to the first ray. The situation of being boss, administrator, manager, project director requires access to first ray energy, generally speaking. The father as the head of one big happy family requires less of that energy. One can, of course, be a father on any ray. Thinking that he was going beyond the cultural role to the archetypal role, he was actually resisting the appropriate first ray energy and substituting the most comfortable role-energy possible to fulfill minimal obligations. Needless to say, he encountered difficulties of a fundamental nature.

Egalitarian or Hierarchical Approach. The storefront institution needed a janitor. The young man Kohl hired for the job worked and played with the kids, discussed and drank with the teachers, and he also swept the floors. "Even though our rhetoric was egalitarian, the situation was hierarchical until we all took the responsibility of cleaning." Once again we see Kohl uncomfortable in the hierarchical situation of having to give orders, of being the boss. To his second ray sense of equality the hierarchical order of things was a disturbance. But "collective cleaning didn't work and later on in the year we decided to take in another janitor." The same pattern repeated itself, however, for this "janitor" also became "part of the group, and we returned to collective though inadequate cleaning."[29] Kohl in his small Other Ways institution was not able to provide adequate maintenance. To some first and seventh ray types this would indicate incompetence. Some very lofty visions and some practical methods of education must have been shared during Kohl's discussion sessions, but in terms of building an organization he was just barely inching his way along.

In his loose family style of organization "problems arose when people failed to abide by collective decisions or acted in the name of the group without telling others what they were doing."[30] When others failed to abide by collective decisions, it was Kohl's position to take administrative action, but he failed to do so. When others acted in the name of the group, it indicated a lack of clarity as to who was responsible for what decisions. The egalitarian approach was clearly not working. Or, if there is a balance needed between the hierarchical and egalitarian approaches, Other Ways was clearly overbalanced in the egalitarian direction. Kohl felt that such matters as not abiding by collective decisions, making individual decisions in the name of the group, talking behind the back of others, and enjoying another's failing, were matters occurring in the old established culture but should not be occurring in the new culture. His colleagues, he felt, simply should not have made such mistakes. The fact is, however, that these problems were occurring and some administrative procedure was required in order to correct them.

To correct the mistakes, however, it was necessary to develop a "new" energy. Kohl tried to avoid the matter through ignoring it, which resulted in the reoccurance of the same problem-pattern.

Kohl placed the responsibility of janitorial duties entirely on the shoulders of the janitor. The janitor was allowed to neglect his duties and still receive his pay check. A second janitor was hired and the same pattern repeated itself.

Creativity and Destructiveness. When giving reasons for not assuming more responsibility, he stated that he was "floundering as much as anyone else." He concluded with the question: "After all, how do you change this incredibly resilient and resistent culture?" When working in Harlem, Kohl noticed the words "Build = Destroy" painted on a wall. Upon enquiring, he learned that the words were from a particular Muslim oriented group. "It meant that an action, in order to effect change, must have elements of both creativity and destructiveness. Neither creativity nor destructiveness is effective by itself."[31] In a certain sense he answered his own question: One changes the culture through a destroying and building process. After developing some teaching principles that put life back into the ghetto children, greatly enhancing their self-esteem and rekindling their joy of learning, Herbert Kohl was shocked to realize that his ideas and methods were not received with open arms by school administrators and other teachers. It was difficult for him to learn that in order for his creative ideas to be implemented on a larger scale some very tenacious obstacles had to be eliminated. The need for destruction came to him as somewhat of an unwelcomed revelation. Creativity alone, he was realizing, was not sufficient. Destruction alone, however, was also not sufficient, for to destroy a harmful program without creating a new program results in being left with "charred ruins" and the likelihood that new construction would simply be "a patched-up version of the old institution."[32] A proper balance between these two elements of creativity and destructiveness was needed. Kohl's ray equipment gave him skill in the creative and visionary areas; the delicate art of destruction was developing much more slowly.

Kohl had the tendency to view destruction in too much of an emotional way. Destruction to him meant yelling, hating, intimidating, arguing, etc. Others were teaching him that destruction meant a non-emotional documentation of facts properly applied through political, organizational and legal processes. There was a tendency for him to get "carried away" and "become impatient." He would sometimes "ruin an opportunity to move someone in power by losing my temper and accusing that person of not caring or of being a hypocrite. My anger in many cases is righteous, but it can be harmful to the group. And my impatience can get on people's nerves."[33] Herbert Kohl realized the need for destruction, or, more appropriately phrased, the need to eliminate certain obstacles whose time for passing had come, but he did not know exactly how to do it.

Staff Factionalized Over Discipline Problem. One of the Berkeley alternative schools had a problem with a thirteen year old student who stayed in the lounge all day and refused to go to classes. Some of the staff wanted her suspended, and another faction said that she "wasn't causing any trouble and had a right to do nothing if she wanted." The disagreement among staff persisted for some time. Eventually the student was suspended, but the "disagreement was never resolved, and the issue of "doing nothing" factionalized the staff for the rest of the year."[34] Many such group factionalizations occur along ray lines. It is very likely that those who opted for the right to do nothing were predominantly along the two-four-six line, whereas those who wanted to take action and expell the student were predominantly along the one-three-five-seven line. Could we say that one way was more correct than another? The situation dealt with a question of discipline-punishment as a result of the breaking of rules. There was a certain ambiguity due to the fact that the breaking of rules was a passive one ("not causing any trouble") rather than an actively disruptive one. Nevertheless, there was a rule infraction that could influence the other students in a negative way. Some action had to be taken. Again, it was the two-four-six type's tendency to avoid an individually painful or "destructive" action (such as firing or expelling) that prevented right response. A right action, no matter how painful, is really designed to preserve the order and well-being of the whole. Needless to say, however, destruction is frequently used merely to preserve a dangerously outmoded status quo. The point here is that an action which is painful to some need not necessarily be a wrong action — something that the second ray and the fourth ray have a particularly difficult time learning. Again we are reminded of the statement in *Esoteric Psychology* that the fourth ray type can fluctuate between "a hatred of causing pain amounting to moral cowardice, indolence, procrastination, a desire to let things be, to rest" on the one hand and a "fiery, impatient, ever urging to action" on the other.[35] Kohl did not want to bring documented evidence causing the firing of a principal and some teachers, even though they were being harmful to the students.

He did not want to fire anybody in his "Other Ways" organization, which resulted then in disorganization and a lack of effectiveness. And here a group of teachers in an alternative school system could not bring themselves to the point of expelling a student, even though there were seeds of much disorder and disruption in the student's noncompliance.

Learning to Negotiate. As well as having various "happenings" and discussion sessions at the store front, Other Ways also went into the classroom with story telling, poetry workshops and various other creative endeavors. Other Ways was generally well-received by the student body and by some parents. Herbert Kohl was definitely having an effect on the Berkeley school system. His grant money, however, was sufficient for one year only, and continuation depended on the Berkeley school board. For the most part, his style, radical and abrasive at times, alienated the administration. His power base was with the students and parents who demanded his continued presence. "When Other Ways was attempting to negotiate with the Berkeley United School District for funds to continue, we found that if the group hung loose, we would be destroyed." When sitting down to talk to the principal or superintendent or "some other bureaucrat", it was necessary that his group "agreed with one another on all points, that we acknowledged a spokesman", and that any anger, walk-outs and threats were prearranged. To avoid "snap decisions that might defeat us", the group agreed to withdraw and discuss the matter in the event of unexpected difficulties arising during negotiations. They learned that "an easy way for a group to be defeated in negotiations is for them to show internal disagreement publicly." The superintendent, they found out, was a master at shifting attention away from himself and to the groups that were confronting him, and then "turning people against one another." "Any sign of weakness can be fatal. We ended up role playing many of the meetings with people who had power over our lives."[36]

At this point Kohl was talking strictly power issues. It wasn't a matter of trying to convince the superintendent that he had a good educational program from a philosophical-educational-psychological point of view. The superintendent wanted him out. Kohl had to fight for his educational existence. And to do so he had to learn to play the first ray power game. In this situation that "game", that energy, is the ruler. He had no alterative but to enter into that energy. Strong philosophically, weak in the ways of power,

Herbert Kohl stumbled along, painfully learning from his mistakes. He was beginning to plan strategic moves. He was bringing his emotional dramatics under control or using them in a calculated way. He was learning how to organize a group, organize support, and speak from the power base of a group. He was learning how to negotiate — and to negotiate not with hatred or disdain but with respect for the other person's position. The first ray type in the position of power tends to realize that if he is too rigid, too inflexible, he stands a very good chance of being toppled from his position. The first ray type also tends to be in touch with several factions, several points of view, and, though expert in none (in the fifth ray sense), he may see validity to all. The two-four-six types, on the other hand, may be so caught up in their special vision of things, that they may tend to disregard other points of view that are necessary balancing factors and that also have a certain validity to them.

Structure and Flexibility. It was Herbert Kohl's observation that some teachers felt that students should have a great deal of freedom, whereas others felt that everything should be "carefully planned and well structured."[37] Generally speaking, the two-four-six types will tend towards a flexibility that gives ample room for spontaneity and creativity. The one-three-five-seven line, dealing with the form factor, will tend toward a planned well-structured approach. (The third ray under certain circumstances can be an exception to this general rule. Combinations of these rays can find a middle path between these two lines of energy.) As well as in the educational setting, Kohl observed that the structure-flexibility polarity also occurred in various groups and organizations. Kohl made the following summation of his observations:

> Some groups decide to be stable, rigidly structured, demanding of absolute allegiance, and completely predictable. Others choose the route of personal whim, spontaneity, flexibility, independent action. The former type of group turns fascist, the latter chaotic. For a group to remain open the complex interplay of both terms of the contraries has to be integrated into its common life. Flexibility has to be balanced by enough structure so that people know what they are responsible for; spontaneity is needed to respond to new situations; logical thought often prevents group

suicide. Personal independence must be respected, but binding collective action sometimes has to be taken.[38]

The polarities line up as follows:

stable	flexible
rigidly structured	personal whim
demanding allegiance	independent action
predictable	spontaneous
fascist	chaotic

Kohl, as we are seeing, moved from the flexible-spontaneous-independent pole towards a more balanced approach. Wanting to leave everyone completely free and independent, he came to realize that "binding collective action" has to be taken. Initially tending to be somewhat of an extremist and tending to polarize, he came to realize that the "complex interplay of both terms of the contraries has to be integrated." We find here then a gradual understanding of the other major line, generally speaking, and significant steps towards wholeness. With pronounced types along the other major line the reverse would tend to be true. The tendency to favor a rigid, predictable system would have to be adjusted to include the flexible, spontaneous and independent.

Although, generally speaking, the abstract two-four-six line is more flexible than the more concrete or form responsible one-five-seven line, the sixth ray can at times be the most inflexible ray. The sixth ray brings the qualities of devotion, strict adherence to an ideal, dedication, and one-pointedness that, in combination with other rays and at a certain point of evolutionary development, can lead to fanaticism. "It will usually be discovered that the man who succumbs to an "idee fixe" has not only a fifth ray mental body but either a sixth ray personality or a sixth ray emotional body."[39]

Wholeness. Kohl makes an interesting distinction between completedness and wholeness. Completedness implies a "final fixed self" and is a "form of death" or a "putting an end to growth." Wholeness, on the other hand, "implies a continuing and evolving responsiveness to the totality of experience one is capable of encompassing." In other words, completedness is a sort of crystallization — a state that changes only through a melting down or separation into constituent parts. But what is it that constitutes a whole? According to Kohl: 'To start with, *wholeness* means being conscious of the different components of one's existence; means keeping social and historical awareness present along with personal and psychological need and insight; means attempting to bind together the internal and external, physical and spiritual, communal and individual aspects of one's life no matter what pain or conflict is involved. This last means breaking away from the dichotomized life that is characteristic of the 'Western' way of living."[40] "Historical awareness" is one way of considering wholeness. As well as individuals evolving, tribes, communities, nations, disciplines or fields of endeavor all evolve. The historical perspective deals with the age or stage of development of the collective. Perhaps Kohl was trying to gain an historical perspective regarding the field of education. Insights, ideals and breakthroughs need time to trickle down to and significantly alter the mass consciousness. If we get too engrossed in our own personal success or personal history, then we may well miss our true role or contribution to the larger whole. The historical development of the discipline is important. One's own personal recognition vis-a-vis the larger picture is far less important.

To recognize wholeness, then, Kohl suggested that we need to be conscious "of the different components" that comprise the whole. Kohl lists some dualities — internal-external, physical-spiritual, communal-individual — but beyond that he does not go. The study of the seven rays, with their complex and rhythmic interweaving of certain basic energies is one way of acquiring a working knowledge of these "different components."

Summary. Herbert Kohl's initial interests were philosophy and education. His success as a classroom teacher led him "quite unexpectedly into political and social conflict." His second and fourth ray energies brought to him a love of teaching, sensitivity to the psychological condition of his students and a creative way of inspiring interest in the curriculum. In dealing with first ray issues and situations he tended to feel his way slowly and blindly along. He got emotionally upset under pressure, failed to plan and failed to use carefully thought-out strategies, prefered the "unprofessional" method of revealing one's feelings (pouring out one's heart), and was unfamiliar with the subtle and necessary art of destruction.

The first thing he did as a means of acquiring something of the first ray energy (albeit unconsciously) was to turn the problem over to others more skilled in this area of the political and then to work with and observe them. His next step was to undertake a project himself that required the use of the first ray energy (again unconsciously, or not realized as such by the personality-brain consciousness). The things of a first ray nature that he learned while working on his project of Other Ways include the following: to conserve energy, to "keep anger from corrupting my work", to do modest work, to take one small step at a time, to be brief, not to be intimidating, to be diplomatic, to be a manager-boss (but initially only as a gracious father figure), to destroy so that creative new forms can come into existence, to politically align himself with others, to develop poise and skill-in-action, to negotiate, to plan meetings, to have a spokesman during negotiations and not to show internal disagreement. He also learned the value of structure as opposed to personal independence.

As a specialist in his particular field of education, he made a significant contribution. As he found the opportunity to expand his work and as he moved into political-social areas, he was brought face to face with his own limitations. In terms of progression towards wholeness this was a very critical point. He could easily have chosen a path of least resistance and remained comfortably and repetitively within the confines of his speciality. He chose, however, a path of resistance which was also a path of special opportunity. He penetrated into a first ray world to which he was fundamentally blind, and he came away from the experience espousing wholeness.

Reed Whittemore: Poet or Journalist. Reed Whittemore, poet and English professor, was hired as a literary editor by *The New Republic* in 1969 — a position that he held for "four interesting years." He had been an English teacher for nearly thirty years before entering the qualitatively different world of journalism.

Initially, the differences were not altogether clear to him. He was hired to be "as literary as I chose in the magazine's back pages." He was simply bringing his extensive knowledge of literature to the editorial position with little anticipation of learning something new. But gradually

> ". . . the journalistic spirit did creep into both my writing and editing, partly because I was working against deadlines and partly because the mere act of working for an essentially journalistic enterprise gave me a journalist's yearnings, yearning to be . . . 'on top of everything' . . . . But for someone like myself bred up in the older faith that one achieves topness mere-

ly by ascending to the top of a thinker's tower and sitting there thinking — that, and reading what earlier tower thinkers thought — for such a person *The New Republic* experience was a novelty. It made me simultaneously aware of how cloistered I had been in the palmy days of my writing for quarterlies and how cloistered I was in another and new sense when riding along with the press and TV (for I became a TV critic too). The articles here[41] reflect the latter cloistering most. They are a record of mind that lived close, for four years, to the doctrine that knowledge and wisdom come to those who are up-to-date and stay there constantly, never letting a fad or fashion or major event slip by unnoticed into the night. I came to fear that doctrine, and to grow nostalgic for the old days of Beauty and Truth, but I came to believe it partly too. Certainly I lived it."[42]

Comparing these two areas of journalism and English teaching he also mentioned:

More than anything else the takeover by journalists of art and the profundities weakened the English teacher's authority since for generations what he had had (or thought that he had had) that the journalists and other new entrepreneurs did not have was Truth and Beauty, plus the myth that Truth and Beauty were eternal, or near enough to the eternal to put those who lived by daily ephemera at a disadvantage. But now someone had intervened to decree that Truth and Beauty inhered to the daily ephemera and not to the eternal.[43]

The polarities and the qualitative differences between these two fields begin to line up. On the side of jounalism we have "being on top of everything", staying constantly up-to-date, being in touch with the "daily ephemera" and never letting a "fad, fashion or major event slip by into the night." On the side of English teaching we have a cloistered thinker's tower concerned with eternal Truth and Beauty. There are obvious form differences between these two worlds. The subtle qualitative energy differences only became apparent to Whittemore after he had stepped out of long experience in one world and entered novice into the other. From a ray point of view, we are dealing on the one hand with a fourth ray or two-four combination concerned with Truth and Beauty, with the creative world of literature and poetry, and with the teaching to others something of this world of subtle psychologies, beauty, sensitivities and values. On the other hand we are dealing with a first ray (or a one-three combination) that is concerned with adaptation to the needs and interests of the time, with the survival of a business, and with being on-top-of or in control of the moment, the present.

It is interesting that working with *The New Republic* made him aware of "how cloistered" he had been in his ivory tower of academia. But after spending some time in his new world of journalism, he came to the conclusion that the world of journalism was cloistered also. In other words, although journalists are up-to-date, on top of the moment, uncovering major events, as well as fads and fashions, they are still unaware of the depth or "profundities" of many of the worlds with which they come in contact. Whittemore in a certain sense is saying that he is shocked at how limited his own world was, but as an outsider in a new world he sees that the phenomenon holds true for them as well. They too are limited. The difference being, however, that Whittemore sees both worlds now, whereas the journalists he encountered for the most part do not. One could say that Whittemore at this point has made a significant step towards wholeness.

There are certain ray similarities between Reed Whittemore and Herbert Kohl. Both were involved in the field of education as teachers, both were creative writers, both loved the abstract world of Truth and Beauty and both were deeply attuned to the worlds of literature and poetry — all of which is strongly suggestive of a fourth ray mind with a second ray influence possibly at the soul level. (This is not to say that all people involved in these areas have a predominance of these two energies. Each case has to be considered individually.) Similar to Kohl, Whittemore moved from a two-four ray setting into a situation where the one-three-seven line was predominant. Unlike Kohl, Whittemore made the entrance into a "foreign" ray situation after *thirty years* of developing and securing his specialty. And unlike Kohl, Whittemore's new field required much of his already developed ray experience. In other words, Whittemore was dealing with a combination of one-four energy as journalist-literary critic. A *thorough* knowledge of the literary art was required as well as the journalistic sense of being on top of the current event (the present crisis situation). It is highly unlikely that a pure first ray type would gather the kind of thorough knowledge of the literary art that Whittemore did.

Although he was moving into a first ray field, his fourth ray experience was indispensible. His new job required a true combination of the one-four energies. Kohl, on the other hand, entered a new field or set of situation-problems where first ray skills were paramount. His profound educational-philosophical knowledge often impaired his ability to take one necessarily small intelligent step at a time. In a certain sense, a smattering of the progressive educational directions along with seasoned administrative skill might have served him better in the task of institutionalizing the new ideas. Whittemore's experience in the foreign ray situation was a much smoother, much more comfortable, much more successful one. It was not nearly so conflict ridden as was Kohl's experience.

Whittemore described the person who hired him as being "old-school" and someone who thought "reporters should be reporters, not singing birds."[44] Are there new schools of journalism that advocate a "singing bird" style of journalism? Or is it not a matter of old and new but rather a matter of type? The phrase "reporters should be reporters" conjures images of tough-minded people knocking down doors to get at the cold, hard facts. "Singing birds", on the other hand, is more suggestive of the ivory tower type, who is more concerned with beauty, with inspiration, with subtle and ornamental phrasing, etc. The cold-hard-fact person is indicative of the first ray type, whereas the singing bird suggests the fourth ray type. The common ground is writing; the styles, in a sense, are in opposition to one another. The singing bird is essentially a poet — an entertainer with hidden meaning or a teacher, a revealer, through beauty. The reporter is one who goes out and gets facts-information and reports them.

On this matter of journalist-versus-poet controversy Whittemore wrote: 'Ezra Pound, an oldtime hater of journalists, put the hex on them once by saying that they had absolutely no minds of their own but functioned only to tell the public what the public wanted to hear. The poet's obligation on the other hand, Ezra Pound hurried to point out, was to tell the bloody public what it did not want to hear." Whittemore thought that Ezra Pound was right. If one did not write what the public expected, one suffered from "having no public." But as well as being "slaves to the public taste," Whittemore discovered that journalists were also "the public's leaders, the public's tyrants of taste . . . . They harkened to the big stories and competed madly with each other in bringing the public the delights of national scandals and tragedies, but they also moved in on the stories and came to govern their destinies. And of course told the public what to think of the stories." Whittemore went on to say that Ezra Pound perhaps failed to see the "enormous authoritarianism" of journalism.[45]

The common ground between these two worlds is the end product of writing, but there the similarity ends. Ezra Pound criticized the journalists for having no minds of their own, no personal opinion, as it were. One could construe from this that Pound probably considered journalists to be non-creative thinkers. But since the qualitative worlds are entirely different one cannot apply the standards of one world to those of another. The journalist is not supposed to have a "mind of his own" in the sense of being an opinionated or creative thinker. The journalist uses his mind in a more practical-active-observing sense. The journalist is looking for facts, and for that he needs skill in contacting reliable sources. The actual writing is not as important as acquiring the accurate, up-to-date and difficult to obtain information. To say that a journalist has no mind of his own in the opinionated-creative sense is analogous to criticizing a pastoral poet for insufficient scientific data or natural history in his poetry. The standard of one discipline (an effect of ray energy) is simply not applicable when appraising another.

One can also note here the tendency of the fourth ray mind to exaggerate as in the characterization of journalists being "slaves" to public taste on the one hand and "tyrants" of taste on the other. The exaggerated word has a shocking or arresting or dramatic effect and is intended to startle the reader out of a bland or nondescript or crystallized way of looking at things. Accuracy is secondary to affecting a change in consciousness through the dramatic (conflicting) means. (Exaggeration can also be used, or should we say misused, as a means of glamorizing and casting a veil over the real.)

Ezra Pound was criticizing journalism *not* as one who had had a long successful career in the field and, therefore, as one who thoroughly understood the field and had a right to criticize, rather he criticized (belittled) journalists out of his own highly developed specialty and out of the prejudice of his own ray type. Whittemore thoroughly understood Pound's position because Whittemore had come from a similar ray situation. He, too, in all his erudition had been "cloistered" from other vitally contributive qualitative worlds. But now, having entered and labored in that field, Whittemore was trying in a sense to set the poet straight. Journalism is not what the poet thinks it is. It is not mindlessness and not slavery. There is a certain adaptation to present tastes and there is also fulfilling a need for information. There is a certain subtle control or governing of the situation through the very fact of reporting or bringing little known facts out into public view. The selection of what facts and what stories to report also deals with the "governing of their destinies."

"Images Pulled out of Air" Versus "Nothing But Flux." While working at *The New Republic*, Whittemore still frequented "poet circles where several sensitive souls never read newspapers at all but measured their days instead by precious images that they personally pulled out of the air and pinned to paper." As he traversed these two "worlds", he worried at times about the preservation of his "own identity." "On the one hand I was trying to set literary fold straight for their failures to write about the society around them, and on the other I was trying to set journalists, and media people, straight, for knowing too much too soon, and for believing in nothing by flux."[46] This is a most interesting observation, for it characterizes clearly the two psychological worlds. He went back and forth between a developed and refined fourth ray (or two-four) world of seeking to tap the intuitive source for artistic expression ("pulling images out of the air and pinning them to paper") and a predominantly first ray world of journalism that deals with knowing as much as one can as quickly as one can about the currently key issues. He had come to a point where he recognized the differences, could function in both worlds colored by different ray energies and could appreciate the reality of both worlds. He had made a significant step towards wholeness. In his effort to set each world straight, he *encouraged the complementary factor that leads towards wholeness*. It is unlikely that he accomplished more than planting a few seeds for possible future growth-expansion through his intellectual clarification. He himself had acquired the expanded step towards wholeness through an immersion in the thought, feeling and activity of a complementary ray. In other words, for all practical purposes, he *became* the other ray, relatively speaking.

Again, it is interesting to see how he characterized these two worlds. The poets never read newspapers and tend not to be concerned with society around them in terms of practical, detailed necessities. (This tends to be true where there is a pronounced fourth ray type, where both the mind and personality are on the fourth ray or where the abstract two-four-six line predominates with an emphasis on a fourth ray mind. This tends not to be true when the fourth ray is complemented by one of the more concrete one-three-five-seven ray energies.) On the other hand, the first ray type tends to "know too much too soon" and to believe "in nothing by flux." In other words, Whittemore as English teacher wrote poetry and articles for scholastic journals. There was a depth of knowledge to his writing; he knew more than what was actually put on paper. Whittemore as journalist and literary editor, however, was in touch with what was current and hot, but often wrote on things about which he had little depth of knowledge. As literary editor for *The New Republic* he also had access to certain lines of communication, to certain sources. Vital information could be gathered quickly, and this was more important in a sense than having knowledge oneself. Access to information is more related to the power factor.

As Whittemore commuted between these two worlds, he was "worried about my own identity and the preservation thereof." He was at a point where he could identify with both worlds — not just superficially but to a significant degree since he had achieved considerable success in both fields. But, interestingly, he could no longer identify quite so completely with the literary world, and, though he could identify with the journalistic world, he could not do so in such a complete fashion as did the journalists around him. So, although he could identify with both worlds, he could not identify with any single one. Having entered another world, he was leaving both behind — thus, the worry about his identity. What world did he belong to? And where were his compatriots? Trying to set the poets straight, on the one hand, and trying to set the journalist straight on the other, he was losing compatriots on both sides. He was beginning to stand alone — stand alone, yet paradoxically as the only one with a true group or holistic sense, relatively speaking.

More Capable of Coping with the World. As a poet, Whittemore was accustomed to writing when "the spirit was upon me." He never did quite get used to writing for "somebody else's spirit." He considered it a discipline, however, that was good for him. Meeting deadlines, staying "on top of articles right through the printing process" was beneficial. He felt that he was becoming "more competent, more capable of coping with the world than I had been when I was merely a grubby teacher writing petulant complaints in student margins . . ."[47]

There are three factors of interest here from the angle of the seven rays. First of all, two kinds of writing are indicated: One deals with inspiration and the other with an intelligent appraising of human affairs. The fourth ray mind tends to be more inclined towards the inspirational, inward search, whereas the first ray mind deals more with the daily issues of necessity, responsibility and power. Inspiration is a delicate matter and one that tends to resist a time frame or the bending to the human will. As Robert Graves put it: "A poet cannot continue to be a poet if he feels that he has made a permanent conquest of the Muse, that she is always his for the asking." If the poet uses "second-hand phrases and ingenious verbal tricks", something that the intellect can accomplish and something that can be put on a time frame and tuned out to meet deadlines, then the Muse "rejects him more decisively even than she rejects the tongue-tied or cowardly bungler."[48] Indeed, Whittemore as poet was accustomed to writing only "when the spirit was upon me." Whittemore as journalist was acquiring a discipline of another sort. He had to write from a different source, a different energy. Instead of inspiration-intuition, he had to find more of a practical-intellectual approach to the problem. The shift was from fourth ray to first ray, or two-four-six line to the one-three-five-seven line.

This leads us to our second point, which is that he now felt "more competent, more capable of coping with the world." Such matters as staying "on top of articles right through the printing process" was illuminating in terms of physical plane problems. The one-three-five-seven line in general facilitates the "coping with the world" in that it concerns itself with the form, thus, the practical, the physical, the concrete. Having acquired something of the first ray energy through his job necessities of dealing with specific and practical problems, he was then able to carry this over into other aspects of his life. Seeing this as a qualitative energy rather than a specific skill, this would necessarily be the case. In other words, a particular practical skill in itself might find no application outside of the shop, but a qualitative ray energy would enable a person to approach a variety of problems with a new perspective. Whittemore's statement that he was now more "capable of coping with the world" is a most significant one in that it marks a "descent" from his academic and poetic thinker's tower to more immediately practical situations. With others it could be just the opposite. Some are so involved in the immediate necessities and practicalities that higher values are lost to sight and materialistic values predominate. Their need then would be time for more abstract, reflective thought on Truth and Beauty, followed by appreciative and creative activity in these realms.

The third point deals with his statement that he was now more competent than when he "was merely a grubby teacher writing petulant complaints in student margins." Here we find the fourth ray mind's tendency towards self-effacement, exaggeration and inaccuracy. Reed Whittemore was an acclaimed poet and professor of English at the University of Maryland. To refer to himself as a "grubby teacher" is as much of a distortion as "grubby editor" or "grubby journalist" would be had he made that self-reference. The distortion serves perhaps to distance himself from his earlier more cloistered attitude. As most exaggerations go, it is a colorful statement and tends to quicken the reader's interest and prevent the mind from falling into a semi-conscious doze as it passes over the written word. The first ray type would tend not to make such an exaggerated, self-effacing comment. Indeed, from a power point of view, a professorship is a position of considerable influence in the community. As a rung on the career ladder it is a significant step. Whittemore was looking at it, however, more from a fourth ray and consciousness angle. He was trying to distance himself from his earlier state of mind — not that he had not been an inspiring teacher, but now he knew so much more in a qualitative sense. It wasn't the position of power and influence that concerned him; it was his level of consciousness. As a means of repulsing that earlier self, he was setting himself in conflict with it.

A missed opportunity. After working at *The New Republic* for three years, Whittemore received a call from "an assistant to a prominent columnist for the *New York Times*" who wanted to be filled in "on the current state of poetry so that she could fill her boss in on it and, in a couple of days, he could toss off a column on it." This was upsetting to Whittemore in that the columnist did not get in touch with Whittemore directly, and, more important, the columnist apparently was going to write an article on poetry without looking at any poetry himself. Whittemore concluded: "I slowly discovered that I could not write about anything; I didn't have the arrogance for it . . ."[49]

The columnist did not know the heart and soul of the subject matter and this was disturbing to Whittemore's two-four sense of things. It was an "arrogant" thing to do. There are first ray ways of doing things that Whittemore still could not comprehend. Once again, in-depth knowledge was not the issue — for that one goes to publications other than a newspaper or magazine. In a newspaper you want quick, up-to-date information that keeps you informed of certain basic trends and certain significant developments in as short a space as possible. What could Whittemore have done in this first ray situation? He could have endorsed a few of his favorite poets. What an opportunity for drawing attention to, say, a young poet of considerable genius but no recognition. He would have been doing his art a considerable service. Also, he could have opened the door of communication between himself and one of the most influential newspapers in the country for a possible future exchange of favors or services. His fourth ray perception of things prevented him from seizing an opportunity that most likely would never come again.

Summary. Reed Whittemore entered the world of journalism with an extensive literary and teaching background. In terms of ray energies, he entered a world dominated primarily by rays one and three from his own background of a relatively developed sense of rays four and two. He was able to function in the "new" world, for as literary editor the two worlds of academic English and journalism overlapped. He had extensive knowledge-energy of one and was forced to acquire (to be) knowledge-energy of the other. He began to see the positives and negatives of both energies relative to their disciplines. Unlike the poets who viewed journalists only in negative terms (no mind of their own, slave to public opinion) and unlike the journalists who viewed poets as ineffectual "singing birds", Whittemore appreciated both energy-worlds. He was achieving a more holistic, comprehensive point of view. This additional and complementary energy-world made him generally "more competent, more capable of coping with the world" — that is, he was more capable of functioning in the practical form world dominated by rays one-three-five-seven. After "four interesting years" in journalism, he returned as a more complete, more comprehensive person. We make the assumption that the four years spent outside of his discipline were of greater benefit than four continuous and additional years would have been, had he never left his area of specialization. We say of greater benefit both in terms of developing a more comprehensive (whole) view of things and in terms of insights-knowledge pertaining to his own specialized discipline. Paradoxically then, knowledge in one's own specialized field can be enhanced by entering a complementary field. This is the principle that Buckminster Fuller discovered and exemplified. And it is a principle of which the rays will help us to gain a scientific understanding.

Buckminster Fuller — A Comprehensivist. Buckminster Fuller wrote: "I am advantaged in many ways in our day, because I deliberately set about in 1927 to discipline myself to be a comprehensivist; thus countering the almost overwhelming trend to specialization. I am quite certain that the most important reason for my having known some success is that I have had no competition."[50] There seems to be a close relation between Fuller's "comprehensivist" and the process under discussion of becoming whole. Fuller attended the U.S. Naval Academy at Annapolis in the early part of World War I. At that time naval officers were "selectively promoted for comprehensive ability." The major reason for this was that radio at the time was not trusted for vital and strategic communications. The naval officer necessarily had a great deal of autonomy, and he was the "supreme authority when at sea." "Qualifications for such supreme responsibility and initiative required magnificently comprehensive training. The midshipmen had to be prepared eventually to be masters under approximately any conditions."[51]

Listing some of the areas in which they had to have comprehensive knowledge, Fuller wrote: "They had to be extraordinarily familiar with world commerce and the broad ranges of technology. They had to know chemistry, physics, mathematics, logistics, ballistics, economics, biology, law, psychology, and engineering. They had to be able to set up powerful industrially tooled naval bases in foreign parts."[52] In the above examples we are dealing primarily with scientific disciplines (fifth ray), with an organizing and synthesizing of knowledge from various disciplines (first and seventh rays), and we are dealing with administrating a complex military enterprise (first ray). The predominance is one-five-seven or one-three-five-seven, although other rays can play an important part in these fields. Of the above mentioned disciplines, psychology approaches the more abstract line of two-four-six.

After the war Buckminster Fuller tried to utilize the principles of comprehensiveness (wholeness) in civilian life.

> I did so because I felt that the great patterns that were developing in relation to an emergent world man

would require comprehensive capabilities, but at the same time could easily be lost sight of — because men's eyes were being focussed only on special parts in special and exclusive places and were failing to see whole integrated systems of socioeconomic techno-evolution and the latter's relationship to earth and universe.

Thus it happened that, for better or worse, I am a professionally trained and persistently active comprehensive viewer of patterns.[53]

There are a couple of terms here that illustrate the theme of wholeness: the "emergent world man", "integrated systems", and "comprehensive viewer of patterns." Yet another key word used by Buckminster Fuller is "synergy."

"Synergy means behavior of whole systems unpredicted by the behavior of their parts taken separately. . . . The words synergy (*syn*-ergy) and (*en*-ergy) are companions. Energy studies are familiar. Energy relates to differentiating out subfunctions of nature, studying objects isolated out of the whole complex of Universe — for instance, studying soil minerals without consideration of hydraulics or plant genetics. But synergy represents the integrated behaviors instead of all the differentiated behaviors of nature's galaxy systems and galaxy of galaxies."[54]

Chemists discovered that they had to recognize synergy because they found that every time they tried to isolate one element out of a complex or to separate atoms out, or molecules out, or compounds, the isolated parts and their separate behaviors never explained the associated behaviors at all. It always failed to do so. They had to deal with the wholes in order to be able to discover the group proclivities as well as integral characteristics of parts. The chemists found the Universe already in complex association and working very well. Every time they tried to take it apart or separate it out, the separate parts were physically divested of their associative potentials, so the chemists had to recognize that there were associated behaviors of wholes unpredicted by parts; they found there was an old word for it — synergy.[55]

According to Fuller then there seems to be the following set of dichotomies:

comprehensivist	specialist
integrated systems	isolated systems
synergy	energy
integrated behaviors	separate subfunctions
associated behaviors	separate behaviors
group proclivities and associative potentials	separate parts divested of associative potentials
behaviors of wholes	parts

Buckminster Fuller's method for becoming whole (a "world man", a "comprehensive viewer of patterns") was initially modeled after his comprehensive training at Annapolis. This principle of trying to see the "group proclivities" was implemented throughout his life. We see it mainly in the interrelation of several sciences — the fifth ray and the seventh ray seem predominant. The seventh ray is a synthesizing ray, and it would also tend to lend a practical or applied scientific emphasis to the scientific temperament. Unlike many scientific types who tend to place reason at the summit of human endeavor, Fuller placed the intuition on a higher level, and it seems that he had a very good working knowledge of it: "It follows that the more specialized society becomes, the less attention does it pay to the discoveries of the mind, which are intuitively beamed toward the brain, there to be received only if the switches are 'on'. Specialization tends to shut off the wide-band tuning searches and thus to preclude further discovery of the all-powerful generalized principles. Again we see how society's perverse fixation on specialization leads to its extinction."[56]

Our three levels once again are (1) integrating energies but proceeding from a personal point of view, (2) loving the other, true group consciousness, (3) being the other, being the whole. Buckminster's approach could be misinterpreted to read that of an intellectually clever man acquiring knowledge of several scientific fields. This, however, would be an inaccurate interpretation, for he goes far beyond intellectual cleverness. The turning point in his life occurred at the age of thirty-two. He had failed in business, was unable to support his wife and daughter, and was considering suicide. For a year he did not speak and spent his time in meditative thought. Emerging from the contemplative withdrawal, he decided to devote his time to the improvement of life on earth. He recognized his earlier mistake of pursuing personal wealth, and now, dedicating his life to humanity, he realized that he would never want for anything. This dramatic shift in intent is strongly suggestive of that level of consciousness called the higher self or soul. Apparently, it made all the difference in his subsequent discoveries and service.

His remarkable achievement in several fields — fields for which he had no formal academic training — suggests something more than an appreciation of "the other." He held several important positions from chief mechanical engineer of the U.S. Board of Economic Warfare to Norton Professor of Poetry at Harvard. His architectural design of the geodesic dome has gained wide recognition. He has written over twenty-five books, including three books of free verse. He held more than two thousand patents. He was an architect, inventor, mathematician, engineer, cartographer, and in a sense poet and philosopher. He gave himself more than twenty such titles. Some say that the only field he did not touch was music.

In the stage of becoming the whole, relatively speaking, a certain achievement in several areas may be evidenced, as in the case of Buckminster Fuller. Here there is not one speciality tacked on to another, but rather an ability to relate areas in an integrative way and on a higher level. Whole systems then emerge that are "unpredicted by the behavior of their parts." It seems significantly indicative of wholeness when the areas related are — from a specialists point of view — quite divergent or totally unrelated. Albert Schweitzer's achievements, for example, in the areas of music, religion, medical science and administration-management speak very loudly of wholeness. It seems to me that it is in this spirit that Robert Muller, a ranking UN official, wrote the following thought:

> It confirmed my old belief that poetry, love, vision, and dream are often infinitely more perceptive in devising the right course of action than scientific, economic, and political considerations. It made me wish that next to each chief of state and in each international organization there should be poets and artists to inspire human guidance with the eyes and the voice of the heart and not solely with reason. Alas, the time is not yet ripe. Among the vast documentation prepared for the world conferences on the seas, water, and the deserts, there are no poems or songs. Among the experts who attend these conferences there are no poets or artists. How sad this is, when

one thinks of all the love the seas, water, and the deserts have engendered in the hearts of humans from time immemorial. What would the great kings of the past, who were surrounded by poets and artists, say if they saw our world run only by experts, scientists, and politicians?[57]

From a specialists point of view one might ask, what in heavens name does poetry have to do with the running of political affairs or with ecological problems? According to Robert Muller: "A world in which a poem submitted to an international conference raises eyebrows is a world that has still a long way to go in its pursuit of beauty, love, and happiness. Poetry and art are not useless: They are the keenest perceptions of the mysteries of life on this planet."[58] Buckminster Fuller, as a "comprehensivist" would have had little trouble understanding the heart of that message.

Albert Schweitzer. As a young student Albert Schweitzer was especially interested in the natural sciences. Some other subjects presented less attraction and more resistance. "In languages and mathematics it cost me an effort to accomplish anything. But after a time I felt a certain fascination in mastering subjects for which I had no special talent."[59] Similar to Buckminster Fuller, Albert Schweitzer seized the opportunity offered by the educational institutions to develop those academic disciplines and qualitative energies that were paths of resistance and steps towards wholeness. It is interesting that Schweitzer experiences a "certain fascination" in mastering those subjects that came with special difficulty. Mastering a subject is, of course, far more than meeting the minimal, introductory requirements. Often students are able to take courses they don't particularly like and even do well in them. But to become fascinated with mastering subjects that initially cost much to accomplish anything suggests something more.

At the University of Strasbourg Schweitzer initially studied theology and philosophy. In the field of theology he wrote the book *The Quest of the Historical Jesus.* In philosophy he had two works published: *The Decay and Restoration of Civilization* and *Civilization and Ethics.* He was also an accomplished musician. At thirty he published his chief contribution to musicology. *Jean Bach: the Musician Poet.*

After his theological studies, Schweitzer entered the field of medicine. He felt a real "eagerness" in setting to work in the natural sciences. "Now at last I was able to devote myself to what

had held most attraction for me when I was at the *Gymnasium*:
I was at last in a position to acquire the knowledge I needed in
order to feel the firm ground of reality under my feet in
philosophy." He characterized the quest for truth in the areas of
history and philosophy as "constantly repeated endless duels
between the sense of reality of the one and the inventive
imaginative power of the other." On the one hand there was "argu-
ment from facts" and on the other there was "skillfully produced
opinion." In the area of philosophy he found men "who had lost
all feeling for reality" and this he found a "little depressing."
Having spent the major part of his undergraduate work in the areas
of music, theology, history, philosophy, and languages, now in
medicine he felt "suddenly in another country." Indeed, he was
entering a world of a different qualitative energy. Now he was
among men who were "concerned with truths which embodied
realities" and who "took it as a matter of course that they had to
justify with facts every statement they made."[60]

Intoxicated as I was with the delight of dealing with
realities which could be determined with exactitude,
I was far from any inclination to undervalue the
humanities as others in a similar position often did.
On the contrary. Through my study of chemistry,
physics, zoology, botany, and physiology I became
more than ever conscious to what an extent truth in
thought is justified and necessary, side by side with
the truth which is established by facts. No doubt
something subjective clings to the knowledge which
results from a creative act of the mind. But at the
same time such knowledge is on a higher plane than
the knowledge based only on facts.

The knowledge that results from the recording of
single manifestations of being remains ever in-
complete and unsatisfying so far as it is unable to give
the final answer to the great questions of what we
are in the universe, and to what purpose we exist in
it. We can find our right place in the Being that
envelops us only if we experience in our individual
lives the universal life which wills and rules within
it. The nature of the living Being without me I can
understand only through the living Being which is
within me. It is to this reflective knowledge of the

universal Being and of the relation to it of the individual human being that the humanities seek to attain.[61]

According to Schweitzer then the dualities between science and the humanities seem to line up in the following manner:

Science	Humanities
Sense of reality	Inventive imaginative power
Argument justified with facts	Skillfully produced opinions
Firm ground of reality	Lost sense of reality
Exactitude and truth established by fact	Creative act of mind and truth in thought
Unsatisfying incomplete knowledge	Purpose and place in universe, knowledge on higher plane
Recording single manifestations	Answers to great questions
Facts about Being	Reflective knowledge of the universal Being

The fifth ray is an obviously significant focal point in Schweitzer's life, and it seems to be the conditioning ray of his mind. He had a love for the natural sciences. Knowledge based on facts gave him a sense of a "firm ground of reality." He was delighted with the exactitudes of science. His theological rather than mystical approach to religion also suggests a fifth ray influence. The pure scientific type, however, would tend towards a pure research that emphasizes an ever greater refinement of detailed and exact knowledge. Schweitzer added little if anything to scientific research. He chose rather to take existing knowledge and make a more extensive and practical application of it. He chose the path of meeting urgent need on the physical plane. Like Gandhi, he was a very practical idealist. Along with the fifth ray then there was either a first ray or more likely a seventh ray influence. A colleague wrote of him that he "supervised every detail in the functioning of his Hospital",[62] which again is suggestive of a developed one-three-five-seven ray influence, generally speaking.

The prejudices, vices and shortcomings of the pronounced one-three-five-seven types seem to have been lacking in Schweitzer's life, which suggests the balancing influence of the two-four-six line and a significant degree of wholeness. When Schweitzer entered the scientific community, he could see the prejudices as well as the assets of his new psychological family, so he could not completely identify with their specialized worlds. He could fully appreciate the realities that "could be determined with exactitude", but at the same time he observed how some of the scientists lacked an understanding of the "universal life" that can be experienced only through the "living Being within." So Schweitzer did not jump to conclusions, he did not prematurely endeavor to give physical and organizational form to an idea, he did not become materialistic or preoccupied with personal power as some one-seven types may be inclined to do. Also he did not negate the abstractions of the religious quest or the endeavor to answer the "great question of what we are in the universe" as some pronounced scientific types are inclined to do. Schweitzer did not "undervalue the humanities as others in a similar position often did." He apparently was not at that personality level in which there is a tendency to exalt one's own type and belittle another. Moreover, we are not simply looking at an example of broadmindedness or a liberal attitude or a willingness to look at seemingly opposing disciplines. *We are looking at significant accomplishments in several fields responsive to different ray energies.* Schweitzer was at home in the humanities as well as in the sciences. He had a profound love of music, was an accomplished musician and an appreciator of the world of art. Unlike Darwin, Schweitzer's "higher aesthetic tastes" did not atrophy with age, and his mind did not become "a kind of machine for grinding general laws out of a large collection of facts."[63] Philosophy and religion were, in a sense developed energies not superficial acquaintances, in his life. Of the two-four-six ray energies, the sixth ray of idealism and devotion was perhaps the most prominent in his psychological equipment.

Conclusion. In the threefold method for acquiring an understanding of the seven ray energies the following correspondences seem to line up:

intellectual familiarization	soul understanding	spiritual will, being
integration	unity	synthesis
developing one's own rays	loving the other or foreign ray	becoming the other rays
projecting one's own ray	observing the group interplay of ray energies	being all the rays relatively speaking
self-consciousness	group consciousness	God consciousness

As we develop our own ray energies, there is the tendency to be attracted to those of similar ray energy and to repulse dissimilar types. The transition to a recognition of the group interplay of ray energies seems to be a long and difficult process. There is the need to recognize how imprisoned we are in a sense in our own psychological world and how we tend to ignore, fear and belittle worlds unlike our own. There is also the need to recognize how we tend to project our world-type and impose our world-type onto others and onto all situations. There necessitates the development of a detached observation of the ray energy needs of the situation-problem itself. Instead of acting from a point of personal wish and desire, one endeavors to see the archetypal patterns at play. The goal and purpose of life shifts from personal achievement to understanding (consciousness) of the nature of things, of life, of Diety. Instead of developing personal quality in order to get, one observes in order to understand. In the soul sense this removes us from the pain-pleasure polarity, since what is personally painful can be soul illuminating.

Following upon the stage of de-centralization and of recognizing the group interplay of ray energies, there occurs the ordeal of being the whole in a relative and manifested sense. This is not a personal decision to acquire a skill or develop a capacity in an individual sense. Rather it is a will-to-wholeness that works through the integrated soul-personality. Initially the personality tends towards a separative specialization and tends to fight against this inner urge towards wholeness. Eventually the integrating soul-personality can learn to read the signs and symbols of the offered opportunity and can cooperate with this super-conscious urge to wholeness.

REFERENCE NOTES TO THREEFOLD METHOD

1. Alice Bailey, *Esoteric Healing* (New York: Lucis Publishing Co., 1953), p. 308.
2. Alice Bailey, *Esoteric Psychology*, I (New York: Lucis Publishing Co., 1936), p. 9.
3. Ibid., p. 316.
4. Carl Jung, *Psychological Types*, trans. H.G. Baynes and R.F.C. Hull (Princeton, N.J.; Princeton University Press, 1971), p. 489.
5. Carl Jung, *Mysterium Coniunctionis*, trans. R.F.C. Hull (Princeton, N.J.: Princeton University Press, 1963).
6. Charles Darwin, *Autobiography* (New York: W.W. Norton and Company, 1969), pp. 27-8.

7.   Sheila Ostrander and Lynn Schroeder, *Psychic Discoveries Behind the Iron Curtain* (New York: Prentice-Hall, Inc., 1970).

8.   Alice Bailey, *Glamour: A World Problem* (New York: Lucis Publishing Co., 1950), p. 4.

9.   Vannevar Bush, *Pieces of the Action* (New York: William Morrow and Co., Inc., 1970), p. 110.

10. Ibid., pp. 74-75.

11. Vennevar Bush, *Science Is Not Enough* (New York: William Morrow and Co., Inc., 1967), p. 52.

12. Bush, *Pieces*, p. 55.

13. Ibid., p. 131.

14. Martin Buber, *Pointing the Way*, collected essays ed. and trans. by Maurice S. Friedman (New York: Schocken Books, 1957), p. 102.

15. Abraham Maslow, *Towards a Psychology of Being* (Princeton: D. Van Nostrand Company, Inc., 1962), p. 212.

16. Ibid., pp. 91-92.

17. Carl Jung, *Mysterium Coniunctionis*, p. 128.

18. Alice Bailey, *A Treatise On White Magic* (New York: Lucis Publishing Co., 1934), p. 429.

19. Herbert Kohl, *Half the House* (New York: E.P. Dutton and Co., Inc., 1974), p. 3.

20. Ibid., pp. 4-5.

21. Ibid., p. 4.

22. Ibid., p. 7.

23. Ibid., pp. 8, 9.

24. Ibid., p. 34.

25. Ibid., pp. 155.

26. Ibid., p. 156.

27. Ibid., p. 156.

28. Ibid., p. 163.

29. Ibid., p. 157.

30. Ibid., p. 167.

31. Ibid., pp. 22.

32. Ibid., p. 23.

33. Ibid., p. 171.

34. Ibid., p. 185.

35. Alice Bailey, *Esoteric Psychology*, vol. I, p. 206.

36. Kohl, *Half the House*, pp. 204, 205.

37. Ibid., p. 252.

38. Ibid., p. 245.

39. Alice Bailey, *Esoteric Psychology*, vol. II (New York: Lucis Publishing Co., 1942), p. 293.
40. Kohl, *Half the House*, p. 113.
41. The articles are Whittemore's best while literary editor of *The New Republic* and published in his book *The Poet As Journalist*.
42. Reed Whittemore, *The Poet As Journalist* (Washington D.C.: The New Republic Book Co., 1976), pp. 5-6.
43. Ibid., p. 4.
44. Ibid., p. 8.
45. Ibid., p. 7.
46. Ibid., p. 9.
47. Ibid., p. 7.
48. Robert Graves, *The White Goddess* (New York: The Noonday Press, 1969), p. 444.
49. Whittemore, p. 13.
50. R. Buckminster Fuller, *Utopia or Oblivion: The Prospects for Humanity* (New York: The Overlook Press, 1969), p. 207.
51. Ibid., p. 207.
52. Ibid., p. 208.
53. Ibid., p. 209.
54. R. Buckminster Fuller, *Synergetics* (New York: Macmillan Publishing Co., Inc., 1975), p. 3.
55. Ibid., p. 4.
56. Ibid., p. xxvii.
57. Robert Muller, *Most of All They Taught Me Happiness* (New York: Doubleday, 1978), p. 142.
58. Ibid., p. 144.
59. Albert Schweitzer, *Out of My Life and Thought* (New York: Henry Holt and Company, 1959), p. 4.
60. Ibid., p. 104.
61. Ibid., pp. 104-5.
62. Frederick Frank, *Days with Schweitzer* (New York: Henry Holt and Company, 1959), p. 4.

THE USE OF THE SEVEN RAYS IN DREAM INTERPRETATION

Tidal Wave Dream: The Loss of a Loved One. Knowledge of the seven rays can shed much light on the archetypal patterns of some of our more important dreams. Case in point is the following dream reported by a thirty-four year old woman.

On the shore overlooking the ocean was an octagon house with large windows on all sides. It was evening. The sun was setting and the colors were very vivid. Entering the octagon house, I saw that it was an institution for retarded children, similar to one at which I had been employed. "S" approached me and started telling me about the camera he was using. He was describing its technical aspects and also the types of pictures he wanted. I started to feel the rigidity of the institution. There was a coldness and sterility to the place. It was oppressive. There was a lack of humanism, a lack of warmth. I felt confined.

I gently pulled "S" by the arm and said, "Come on, let's go outside." I pointed out the sunset to him, the beautiful colors. I showed him how he could frame the picture with his hands — a living picture. "You see how beautiful it is?"

"S" asked me if I had heard the news. I hadn't. There had been an earthquake in Japan. There was supposed to be a tidal wave heading in this direction. "Let's go down and look at the waves," I said. When we got down to the water's edge, everything went black. "S" grabbed my arm and said, "Hold on tight!" We were swept out to sea and "S" slipped away. I swam around and dove down looking for him. I was amazed to see how strong I was in the water and how well I could swim.

I felt something. An arm. I assumed it was "S"'s, and I struggled to bring him to the surface. Reaching the surface, I started to swim, and the main thought in my mind was: I hope I'm swimming in the right direction towards shore.

When I got to shore I saw that the person I had pulled

out wasn't "S" but my fifteen year old son. I tried to revive him. I grabbed him around the chest and frantically pressed. But he was dead and I had the terrible feeling that there was nothing that I could do.

Interpretation: The Developed Fourth Ray, the Need for the Fifth Ray. There are two rays represented in the dream: "S" represents the fifth ray of scientific knowledge, and "N", the dreamer herself, represents the fourth ray of harmony through conflict. The fourth ray is the stronger element. The dreamer is focussed within a fourth ray point of view. She looks out at the world through fourth ray eyes. "N"'s ray equipment is as follows: Soul II, Personality 7, Mind 4, Emotion 6 and Physical 3. The mental body is the most prominant point of focus at this time.

We see the fifth ray initially through her fourth ray focus. She considers the fifth ray in the form of "S" to be preoccupied with technical questions and to be missing the more important humanistic ones. That is, from her fourth ray point of view, there is a certain coldness and sterility to the fifth ray, a certain lack of livingness, a lack of involvement. From "N"'s point of view, "S" needs to be pulled out of the institutional environment. "N" feels that she has much to teach "S".

She takes him out then into a more living or whole world. She shows him how he can take "living pictures." With her method there is far less technical analysis. There is no separation or removal from the natural flow of life or from the ecological setting. She tries to impart to him a sensitivity to beauty, an involvement with rather than an analytical separation from the environment.

This is the initial setting. The fifth ray is seen primarily critically or in a negative light. The fourth ray is seen in a positive light. The fourth ray focus is trying to impose its vibration onto the unit representing the fifth ray. There is no effort to understand or appreciate the fifth ray. Thus, a crisis is precipitated, which is to say that the stage of development is ripe for a new opportunity, an expansion of consciousness.

"S" or the fifth ray unit reports that a tidal wave may be approaching. From a fifth ray point of view it would be reasonable to seek a place of *higher ground*, that is, some mental distance from the pending emotional (ocean, watery element) crisis. "N", the dreamer, however, is the one in the power or controlling position. The fourth ray attitude is the one then making the decisions. Her decision is to go to the water's edge, which can be a balanced position between mind and emotion, but in this case it is a ludicriously dangerous position. With an approaching tidal wave it is not a *reasonable* position to maintain. And, of course, it cannot be maintained. Standing at the water's edge, the water quickly and imperceptably engulfs them. Darkness ensues, that is, consciousness is lost, or a clear mental focus is not possible within the turbulance of the emotional condition. They are swept out to sea. She loses contact with "S" — the fifth ray factor that could help her attain a clear mental focus. The dominant fourth ray note chooses to *experience* through immersion in the crisis rather than to observe in a detached fashion. The fifth ray "S" cannot *swim* (maneuver on the emotional plane) nearly so well as the fourth ray "N". "N" herself is amazed at how strong she is in the emotional element during the crisis, the conflict.

The outcome of the crisis is most interesting and most instructive. She thinks she is retrieving "S" from the water, but "S" has turned into her son. She tries frantically to revive her son but is unsuccessful. Losing an *acquaintance* in the form of "S" is one thing, but losing her son, her own *flesh and blood*, is quite another. In the initial setting the fifth ray qualitative energy was viewed primarily in a negative way. The effort was made to change the fifth ray element into the fourth. The pronounced fourth ray element precipitated a crisis. The crisis was such that the fifth ray element was lost. And also the crisis revealed how near and dear to her the fifth ray element is.

What is required here then is a change of attitude towards the fifth ray energy. "N" ought to care for it and nurture it as she would her own son. (In the "subjective" analysis of the dream where all factors are part of oneself, rather than the "objective" analysis where things are external to oneself, "S" and her son are part of herself. This is not a dream about her son. This is a dream about a particular quality embodied in the aquaintance "S" and transformed into her son for the purpose of *teaching through analogy*. Thus, this quality is as near and dear to her as her own son, which is a recognition that comes with some shock or only through crisis.) She can lose or fail to develop that needed fifth ray detachment and observation and mental focus if she insists on plunging into those situations where there is emotional turbulence. Emotionally she is strong, sensitive and caring. She has acquired strength, sensitivity and humanistic concern through plunging into and emerging out of a great variety of emotional experiences. Her developed fourth ray mind has enabled her to make very fine differentiations in this watery element, and as a result she has become a very good psychologist. At this point, however, an entirely new outlook towards the fifth ray of scientific knowledge ought to be most carefully considered. Past patterns, although proven successful, need to be eliminated and new patterns need to be developed. This is difficult since there is the tendency to rest on developed past patterns rather than go through the ordeal of change. And it is also difficult in this case, because "N" does not have any fifth ray in her equipment. We are reminded, however, of D.K.'s words that we ought to study the rays which are lacking in our equipment in order that a needed balance (whole) be achieved (*DNA*,I,p.351, 379-80, 134, *Eso. Psych.* II,p.359). In other words, "N" has progressed far along the development of her own ray equipment and along the two, four, six line. She has developed the mind, integrated to some degree the personality and is aligning with the soul. She has many talents and gifts, has a strong influence on her environment, and endeavors to be of service to others. The prompting to develop fifth ray attitudes suggests an opportunity to begin a new cycle of growth.

Dream of the New House. Two or three nights after the tidal wave dream, "N" had another dream that seems to shed additional light on the fourth and fifth ray energies working out in her life.

I dreamed that I was in "my house", the one I'm living in now. A woman with a small baby knocked on the door and said, "Can I come in and say good-bye to the house?" "Sure," I said, "Come on in. My name is "N"." She stared at me and said, "I don't care what your name is. I just want to say good-bye to the house. I used to live here." She seemed very strange. She put her baby on the floor and massaged it as she looked around the room.

I went upstairs. It was a huge house. Much larger than I had realized. I went into a room. It was a beautiful and very spacious room. Just perfect for "Z"'s nursery school. I called down the hall for "Z". She came and I showed her the room. "Look at this room and all these toys! Isn't this just perfect for you? And so spacious!"

The house, even though I was living there, was new to me. There were so many rooms to explore. "Z" and

I went down the hall and into another room. This we quickly realized was "S"'s room. We couldn't resist looking around the room at his things. "S" is a wine taster. There was a large assortment of wines. Then we saw a whole array of health foods. This was a surprise to us. We didn't know that he was into health foods. There was an assortment of herb teas, also a variety of whole wheat pastas and many other things. We were very happy to see this. There was a depth to him we hadn't recognized. We were happy to see this because we felt it would do him a lot of good.

Then I asked "Z", "Did you see that woman downstairs? Isn't she strange? I think she's insane." Just then the woman appeared in the doorway. I looked at her. There we stood face to face. And then I woke up.

Interpretation of Dream. The insane woman and the dreamer "N" are all part of the same subjective life. The insane aspect "used to live here" but doesn't live here anymore. It is a nostalgic visit for her. The insane aspect is the one that in the past has led at times a crazy and wild life. The fourth ray type can reach some dramatic highs and lows. There can be great excitement, much experience and rapid growth. There can also be a tendency towards insanity. The subject "N" has passed through this period with a wealth of emotional-psychological experience. She is now a warm, strong person who aspires to greater knowledge and to be of service to others. But there is a nostalgia involved here. And there is the baby. She massages the baby on the floor. In other words, "N" treats her emotionally extravagant past with a certain amount of affection. She coddles it in fond reminiscence.

"N" leaves this woman to explore *large new rooms* in her house. There has been an *expansion in consciousness*. There is a large new room ideal for a nursery school or for new thought-life to grow. The keynote is joyous new growth. There are toys or a rich assortment of new ideas to play with. The fourth ray *loves to play* with ideas as well as with emotions. A rich imagination and a creativity are the elements of play. Associated with "Z" is a patient, loving, nurturing quality so essential for caring for the very young. "N" has recently been introduced to esoteric psychology, and it seems that this has much to do with the more expansive upper storey of her house and with the new ideas to nurture and with which to play.

They enter into "S"'s room. There is an assortment of wines, for "S" is a wine taster. Here again we have indicated the fifth ray or scientific type in the form of "S". A wine/taster, however, is actually an interesting blend of both fourth and fifth ray energies. The wine taster must identify the form aspect accurately, as the fifth ray so expertly does. The method employed, however, is one of an internal, subjective, personal experience, which is more indicative of a fourth ray approach. The indication here, it seems to me, is that "N" has employed the fifth ray energy to a degree but only in some "wine-tasting" or essentially *intoxicating* experiences. In other words, certain situations were of such a nature that in order to experience and savour them, yet at the same time to avoid the intrinsic danger of them, there was required a mental clarity and analysis of a fifth ray approach. Being a developed fourth ray mind, she readily combined the two energies. The surprise factor (indicating a new recognition) in the dream is that "S" not only has an assortment of wines but he has an array of health food products as well. The recognition is that the scientific energy can be employed in ways hitherto not realized. These new ways do not have the seeds of danger or intoxication to them, rather they have the seed of healthy, psychological growth. So, "N"'s house is now larger with many more rooms. There is an expansion of consciousness, which includes many new ideas to nurture and play with, and which includes to "N" a surprisingly *new use of the fifth ray energy.* She is no longer equating the fifth ray energy with sterile, technical observation within an inhuman institution. She is beginning to see that she can blend it with her already finely developed fourth ray mind and that it can be employed in a variety of daily and psychological-food-for-growth situations.

At the end of the dream, she stands face to face with the insane woman. She has gained distance from this aspect of herself, but nevertheless she must come to terms with it. Truly, the insane woman is a stranger in this house. There is no room for her in this house. She used to live here, but now she doesn't even want to know "N"'s name. Equating *name* with one's *basic identifying energy,* the insane woman finds no vibratory energy with which she can synchronize. But the fourth ray "N" in humanistic fashion extends her hand to the woman. "N" allows a certain "space" to the nostalgic visiter. What is needed here is a first ray ability to eliminate or destroy those aspects of ourselves that are a threat to growth and expansion. The face to face confrontation suggests that this aspect will, indeed, have to be confronted.

THE THREE RAYS
OF ASPECT AND STAGES
OF DEVELOPMENT

One way of considering the three rays of aspect is to see them in terms of a cyclic unfoldment from youth to maturity — from the building of the new form, to the development of consciousness, to the control of that form and consciousness through the will. Charles Leadbeater discussed the "Three Outpourings" of Diety in his book *Man Visible and Invisible.* The sequential unfoldment of the Trinity is first of all the Third Aspect, secondly the Second Aspect, and thirdly the First Aspect. The Third Aspect deals with the "first movement towards the formation of the system." After the form aspect has been somewhat developed, the Second Aspect "descends" or incarnates. This facilitates the "ensouling" of the form or the development of consciousness until on the "upward arc" it meets the third Great Outpouring or the First Aspect, where the factor of will comes into play more dominantly. These aspects seem to be related to rays one, two and three, and they also seem to relate to the manifestation and evolutionary development of all life-forms. Therefore, looking at it from one angle we have the sequential manifestation of first of all the third Ray of Intelligent Activity (form-appearance), then the second Ray of Love-Wisdom (quality-consciousness), and finally the first Ray of Will or Power (life-will), which also seems to hold true in an archetypal sense in the life stages of a human being. First of all there is the *activity of youth*, the development of the physical form (also the development of the subtler forms of the emotional and mental bodies) and the quickening of the *intelligence* factor. Secondly, there is the *middle-years* during which time there tends to be less physical activity and a deepening of subtle consciousness awareness. The self-centeredness of youth is gradually replaced in some degree by group consciousness. Thirdly, there is the stage of *maturity*, which is characterized by the responsibility of power. Each of these three stages could be divided into three sub-stages, which could be diagramed in the following manner:

Years	Sub-Cycles and Ray-Aspects	Cycles and Ray-Aspects	
63 ___ _____			
	1		Maturity
54 ___			
	2	1	Purpose-Will
49 ___			
	3		
42 ___ _____			
	1		Middle-Years
35 ___			
	2	2	Consciousness-Quality
28 ___			
	3		
21 ___ _____			
	1		Youth
14 ___			
	2	3	Activity-Form
7 ___			
	3		
0 ___ _____			

The period from 0 to 7 would be the activity sub-cycle of the activity major cycle. *Physical activity* and the building of the *physical mechanism* would receive the major thrust of the evolutionary and developmental forces. From 7 to 14 the *emotional body* would be the area of special focus. During this second sub-cycle of the *activity* cycle, emotions would be in their formative stage. And also being the *second* sub-cycle of the activity cycle, it would be the sub-cycle focusing on the factor of consciousness, which relative to this level would be sentience, feeling, emotion. The power sub-cycle (14-21) of the activity major cycle (0-21) would bring in the factor of the first aspect related to the first ray. Thus, from 14 to 21 the focus of development would shift from the emotional to the *mental* unit, archetypally speaking. The first aspects and the first ray are synthesizing factors. Thus, the first aspect includes consciousness (second aspect) and activity (third aspect) to some degree. The first real awakenings to the need to take *responsibility* and *direction* for one's life would occur during this time. The development of the intellect or lower concrete mind would also occur during this time. This first exercise of power in the activity major cycle could manifest as a confrontation with established units of power (family, school, church, community) and could express itself as a sort of experimental delinquency. The activity factor would still be the main focus. Thus, youths during this stage would *do* things that startle or confront the established power structure, and it would be a doing that preceded thinking or a doing that lacked seasoned thought. There might not necessarily be a rebellion against power structures. The youth could also come to better understand the power structure during this time and cooperate with it.

The middle-years (21-42) would see generally a development and refinement of the consciousness or second aspect. The first sub-cycle (21-28) would be the activity (third ray) stage. During this sub-cycle one would expect the *activity of consciousness* to be evidenced. In other words there very well could be a tendency to develop the intellectual faculties, to read widely, to actively pursue a wide range of fields and subject matter prior to settling down into more specialized or in-depth areas. Also during his time the activity of travel, of acquiring knowledge of diverse cultures, might also be evidenced. There might also be a tendency to go from job to job, actively touching upon broad and diverse fields of endeavor. Thus, the consciousness aspect would be developed and, initially, through active and diverse means.

The second sub-cycle (28-35) would bring in the second ray factor during the middle or consciousness aspect. Thus, it would be both a second ray factor in the larger cycle and sub-cycle. At this time we would expect to see a more profound development of the consciousness factor and a diminishing of activity. One would go deeper into certain fields of special interest instead of jumping from field to field touching only the surface of things, relatively speaking. The first sub-cycle (21-28) would witness the active and eager youth desiring quick success and viewing primarily the activity-appearance-form aspect of life. A deeper, more seasoned, more reflective attitude would be the focus of development in this second sub-cycle (28-35). Archetypally speaking, one would endeavor or have the opportunity to touch the *heart and soul* of a particular area of special interest. One would begin to sense those subtler things that cannot easily be articulated. The abstractions of one's discipline would come to light. The vision of a particular discipline would gradually unfold.

Another factor in this sub-cycle deals with the interplay between the *individual and the group.* The individual is more akin to form-activity, whereas group is more akin to consciousness. During this cycle greater adjustments would be made in respect to the sense of group. The life greater than one's own individual uniqueness would be recognized in a new way. There would be a greater effort and ability to understand others, instead of the demand to be understood. There would be a greater regard for others, instead of a disregard. The struggle, however, to go from an acute individualistic attitude to a sense of group awareness can be frought with turmoil and conflict. The difference between this sub-cycle and earlier ones is that the conflict is more of an inner one, more in the realm of consciousness than in outer activity. One confronts others less, and one in "quiet desperation" confronts one's own concepts and values more.

The third sub-cycle (35-42) would be a more responsible one, bringing in the first ray factor. Here one would have to make some commitments that would condition the remainder of one's life. Dreams are made more practical. Bridges are necessarily burned behind one. Activities are necessarily limited or more concentrated. Key decisions and choices are made. One can no longer include so many possibilities. Which direction will one choose? It can be a matter of grave responsibility and much soul searching during this first ray sub-cycle of the second ray major cycle.

The next cycle (42-63) would witness the emergence of maturity, the inheritance of positions of power, the necessary assuming of positions of responsibility. The first sub-cycle (42-49) is the activity sub-cycle in which the third ray factor would tend to be more visible. In fact during this sub-cycle we might see the individual being particularly active. This activity, however, is vastly different from the activity of youth, for it is less experimentally and adventuristically scattered, and it is more purposefully focussed and directioned. An apparently "new beginning" could occur at this time, such as a new business, a new line of work, some sort of new enterprise. It would in fact not be new in terms of knowledge, interest, field and subject matter. What would be new would be the assuming of certain positions of control and decision making. The third ray under the auspices of the first ray, so to speak, can be a very visibly powerful factor. The next two sub-cycles (49-54 and 54-63) would tend to be less in the public eye and more of a behind-the-scenes labor. The activity of power then could be more directed through others. Here we find one's quiet zenith, which generally then is also the beginning of one's decline. This zenith could also simply be the running of the affairs of a household with dignity, harmony, and organization, or the responsibility of fulfilling of one's job obligations in a reliable way.

The Analogy of a Business Career. Very briefly these three stages or cycles of youth-activity (3rd aspect), middle-years or consciousness-deepening (2nd aspect), and maturity or power-responsibility (1st aspect) could be considered in an analogous way from the point of view of a career in business. During the first stage of Activity-youth (third aspect) one would start "at the bottom", that is, at the most peripheral, most active, most visible or obvious point. Here one would gain some knowledge of what the business *does*. One gains familiarity first of all through doing, through activity. It is a time of testing and of being observed. At the peripheral point one's responsibilities are relatively minor, and one's sphere of influence is a relatively small one. The decisions one makes effect a relatively small population. Yet there is much activity and much busy-ness.

During the second stage of the development of the aspect of consciousness (second aspect) one would begin to move up the ladder, so to speak, away from the most peripheral points, and one would begin to see the business from a new perspective. This might include more education, more training. It might include a promotion to a middle-management position. One of its most essential functions would be to *relate* the directing powers of the business (first aspect) to the activities of carrying out the directives (third aspect). The relationship would be a two-way one. That is, middle management (second aspect) would also convey information to the directing powers (first aspect) concerning the activities and state of affairs occurring at the activity level (third aspect). During this second stage one would have to gain step by step a comprehensive awareness (consciousness) of everything relating to the business. If one simply and actively carried out the orders of others, one would remain at the activity level.

The third stage would deal with entering into the world of the major responsibilities and risks of the directing powers or top executives (first aspect). One could then possibly either stay with the company, entering its higher brackets, or one could go off on one's own and start a new company, being oneself the directing, motivating force. The first ray or aspect, being a synthesizing aspect, has knowledge of and, in a sense, includes the other two aspects.

The Various Cycles and One's Individual Rays. Would one's individual ray equipment predispose one towards an affinity or lack of affinity with and consequent utilization or lack of utilization of a particular developmental sub-cycle? A person, for example, with a first ray mind and a third, fifth or seventh ray personality might tend to have difficulty with the reflective, consciousness-developing sub-cycle of 28-35. The young person along the 1-3-5-7 line entering the competitive job market during the 21-28 sub-cycle might tend to fare better during this activity sub-cycle than those along the 2-4-6 line, broadly and generally speaking. The 1-3-5-7 type would tend to have more of a practical and, in a sense, "realistic" attitude and orientation towards the world of affairs than the 2-4-6 type. A fifth ray influence could very well direct that practical attitude more into academic and technical activity. The following sub-cycle (28-35) might prove more problematical to the 1-3-5-7 type. Power and success generally do not come by the age of 28. Yet certain successes generally do come about. The tendency could be to continue in the same mode, but since the world is not made up of reasoning-activity alone, one would generally run into problems and crises apparently designed to bring about a deeper understanding, a more inclusive consciousness. If the deeper insights are not brought about during this time, then crystallized, unchanging, materialistic thought might predominate, which can also bring about certain types of physical disorders.

A person's development is more cyclic than linear. In other words, right development requires periods of inner withdrawal and reflection as well as periods of activity and expression. A career oriented person, however, tends to imagine a linear progression from one job to another, or one visible mark of achievement to the next, one promotion to another, etc. Periods of withdrawal seem to connote for some the failure of dropping out, when in fact they might be much needed periods of reflection leading to consciousness expansion. The 28-35 sub-cycle then might be very confusing to the 1-3-5-7 type when his whole career as viewed in a linear fashion seems to be threatened.

In the case of the pronounced 2-4-6 type the response and style is generally quite different. Instead of a relatively practical and realistic orientation, we might find a more idealistic or mystic or glamorized notion of life. There might also be evidenced a more creative and iconoclastic life-style and less of a practical career or conventional orientation. There might be a greater willingness to go from job to job of little responsibility rather than climb the vertical ladder of success, which also entails much responsibility. There might also be academic achievement within certain types of institutions and study courses.

The 2-4-6 type tends to take the following sub-cycle (28-35) more in stride and with less puzzlement than does the 1-3-5-7 type. "Drop-out", reflection, withdrawal, flexibility, understanding, tend to come with relative ease to the 2-4-6 type, generally speaking, since these are the rays of abstraction. The 2-4-6 type can blend with and utilize this period, but they may also be neglectful of the more responsible issues they have yet to face. The 1-3-5-7 type may tend to be somewhat restless during this period in which there is a lack of synchronization between the individual's own rays and the key-note of the sub-cycle. This type truly wants to be more directly involved with the business of achievement, with affecting the structure of things, with power-responsibility, than with profundity of understanding that in a form-appearance sense may appear to lead nowhere.

The 28-35 sub-cycle of reflective withdrawal might also witness a settling down and withdrawal into a home life, including the bearing of children, which may be in marked contrast to a more active sexual and romantic life-style of the activity sub-cycle (21-28). Also in the activity sub-cycle there seems to be a need for meeting many people, whereas in the following sub-cycle (28-35) the tendency moves towards close relationships with a few friends.

The will sub-cycle (35-42) forces one to come to terms with certain issues and to make commitments towards certain goals that will culminate only during the will major cycle (42-63). This may cause some consternation for the 2-4-6 type who does not like to deal with first ray issues and who tends to play in this regard a more passive and dependent role. The 1-3-5-7 type, on the other hand, might tend to forge ahead on projects and schemes that are still somewhat weak from a second ray (sensitivity, consciousness, wisdom) point of view. The 1-3-5-7 type might, therefore, work towards a goal that tends to be too materialistic. In the process they might shut off the possibility of further consciousness-expansion of soul illumination and pour all their efforts into the material enterprise.

Generally speaking, the pronounced ray type along one of these two major lines (2-4-6 or 1-3-5-7) is not as common as the blending of these two lines in some ray combination. If there is a blending, then a particular sub-cycle may offer the opportunity for particular work on a particular ray and particular vehicle. To our first hypothetical example of a first ray mind and a third, fifth or seventh ray personality, let us further suppose a second ray soul. In such a case the late twenty's and most of the thirty's would provide a most favorable time for alignment with and development of soul consciousness. The integration of the two major lines could then occur both with a degree of outer success or influential impact and inner awareness or wisdom in the subsequent major cycle of the will (42-63).

The theme apparently is balance, homeostasis, and wholeness. Working against this theme are the tendencies towards inertia, love of ease and comfort, partial success, and mistaking the part for the whole. Crises of a physical, emotional or mental nature tend to alert us to the need for change, which may in many cases include the need to enter into the life-consciousness of a particular ray energy at some level. This can at times ·be an intense and excruciating labor, but it can lead to health, harmony and wholeness.

THE THIRD RAY OF
INTELLIGENT ACTIVITY
CONTRASTED WITH RAYS
FOUR AND FIVE

Words in Their Esoteric Sense. The third ray has been called the Ray of Intelligent Activity. The term "intelligent activity" seems to signify little in itself, for one wonders if everything could not be called "intelligent activity" in some way or another. For example, certainly the work of, say, an eminent scientist who furthers a particular field of study through original research and new discovery could be called "intelligent activity" as this term is generally used. Strictly speaking, however, pure scientific research is not *intelligent activity* in the esoteric sense. This may become clearer if we realize that the third ray is also associated with the third major law, the Law of Economy. This Law deals with such matters as "the line of least resistance", "manipulating matter", and "adaptation."[1] In exoteric terminology and related to the esoteric, "economy" deals with such matters as the most efficient, most utilitarian, most frugal usage of material resources. Pure scientific research is not economic, frugal nor efficient in and of itself. The law of economy (in a certain sense) and the energy of *intelligent activity* may be applied to the discoveries, the results, of pure scientific research, and, thus, a melange of useful products can be manufactured and marketed. But scientific research in itself is necessarily inefficient in terms of motion, of use of materials, of time for observations and data-collecting, etc., and therefore is not *intelligent activity* in the esoteric sense. The true fruit of science is *knowledge*, and, although the fifth Ray of Scientific Knowledge and the third Ray of Intelligent Activity are closely related, they are also distinctly different energies.

Similarly, 'the artistic type, full of the sense of beauty and creative aspiration"[2] is not concerned with economy of activity, although a given artist could appropriately be referred to as "intelligent" in the general use of that word. The labor to bring forth a work of beauty, a work of art, is as time-consumingly inefficient as the labor of pure science is in bringing forth a new discovery, and therefore could not be designated *intelligent activity* in the esoteric sense.

The *activity* of a businessman, on the other hand, must necessarily be *intelligent* to some degree, or he will very quickly go out of business. But again, this is in the esoteric sense as it refers to energies and forces. Thus, a businessman may or may not be "intelligent" in the general use of the word, but nevertheless the third ray energy of *intelligent activity* is very likely to be playing upon and through the man-of-affairs, the accomplished entrepreneur.

Interpretation, Revelation of Meaning, Analysis-Clarification. Bearing in mind the fact that we are using certain key-words in an esoteric sense or as "designators of energy" rather than descriptive of form, it might be helpful to contrast rays three (Intelligent Activity), four (Harmony through Conflict) and five (Scientific Knowledge) in terms of *interpretation, revelation of inner meaning*, and *analysis-clarification*. To *interpret*[3] something is to explain it in an intelligent way, or to provide a one-to-one correspondence, such as interpreting from one language to another or one level of understanding to another. The interpreter is an agent, an explainer, a transmitter, *an adapter*. There is generally something vital and something immediate about interpretation, and therefore, interpretation and *communication* are very closely related.

To *reveal the inner meaning*[4] of something is a phrase used to approximate a process that uses an altogether different energy than interpretation. "Revelation" is generally associated with making matters known in a supernatural manner or with an "enlightening or astonishing disclosure" (*Webster's Dictionary*). Whereas *interpretation* draws on the intellect, the *revelation of meaning* requires a spark of the intuition. Whereas interpretation uses a one-to-one correspondance and explanation, the revelation of meaning relies on imagination, word-pictures and analogy. Whereas the interpretation of truth can be explained and cummunicated point by point, the revelation of meaning requires more of a creation of a holistic experience. Thus, the philosopher *interprets* and the artist *reveals*.

To *analyze* and *clarify* something is neither interpretation nor revelation. In order to make something perfectly and precisely clear, it is necessary to analyze. The opposite of clarity is vagueness and confusion. When a particular part is mistaken for another part, confusion results. In order to be perfectly clear about a particular matter or issue, it is necessary to analyze, to separate, so that each part is clearly seen as a factor in and of itself — so that when one is talking about a particular part, for example, one is not confusing it with some other part. Each part generally requires further and further separation and analysis, which leads to the discovery of finer and finer parts, which leads, then, to greater clarity of knowledge. But it also leads to a technical terminology of very fine differentiations, which results in problems of communication.

The developed scientific fifth ray type tells you what he *knows it is*. Knowing in this sense is certainty and it is what can be proven to others. There is a difinite limit to what one can know with scientific clarity. A great many things happen in the world and in the universe about which we are not able at this point to have scientific knowledge. Nevertheless, in spite of the fact that we cannot *know* something scientifically, we must *interpret* and we must undertake *intelligent action*. Therefore, as the fifth ray type tells you what he knows it is, the third ray type tells you what he *thinks it is* and makes an intelligent, interpretive appraisal. In a certain sense, the intelligent interpretation precedes scientific investigation. As Will Durant wrote: "Every science begins as philosophy and ends as art; it arises in hypothesis and flows into achievement. Philosophy is a hypothetical interpretation of the unknown (as in metaphysics), or of the inexactly known (as in ethics or political philosophy); it is the front trench in the siege of truth. Science is the captured territory; and behind it are those secure regions in which knowlege and art build our imperfect and marvelous world. Philosophy seems to stand still, perplexed; but only because she leaves the fruits of victory to her daughters the sciences, and herself passes on, divinely discontent, to the uncertain and unexplored. Shall we be more technical? Science is analytical description, philosophy is synthetic interpretation."[5] (Two of the special virtues of the Third Ray of Higher Mind as given in *Esoteric Psychology*, I, are: "Wide views on all abstract questions, capacity for concentration on philosophic studies."[6] Philosophy is given as one of the methods of development for the third ray type of Higher Mind.[7])

If the fifth ray type tells you what he *knows it is*, the third ray type what he *thinks it is*, the fourth ray type tells you *what it is like*. The fourth ray type does not tell you what something is with certainty, and he does not interpret things for you with a one-to-one correspondance or with clear intellectual clarity. He does *imply* what something is or tell you *what something is like*, and therefore relies on a subtle art form or on analogy. At one level the fourth ray type endeavors to give you a feeling for the whole of things or the experience of things. The fourth ray type endeavors to go beyond the limitations of the form nature and bring something through, *reveal* something, so that the form nature is substantially changed, inspired, as it were, by something of the formless. "Beauty", according to D.K., "is as much of divinity as can be expressed through any one form"[8]

The intuition, on the other hand, is *not* the exclusive domain of the fourth ray type. Certainly the fifth ray type can be inspired by a spark of the intuition that illuminates a particular line of research. Also an elucidating interpretive third ray explanation can result from an intuitive experience as well. The point here is that the method or technique of the fourth ray type, being the *revelation* of inner meaning (as contrasted to interpretation and analysis), is more directly and persistently concerned with the world of abstraction and, therefore, tends to cultivate the feeling-intuition or the astral-buddhic link.

Similarly, we can say that the mental world of intelligence is not the exclusive domain of the third and fifth ray types. Yet the methods of *interpretation* and *analysis* are more directly concerned with the worlds of concretion (form, activity, law), and therefore the will-mind-form or the atma-manas-physical line tends to be cultivated.

Beauty or the revelation of inner meaning is a subtle and evasive matter. It satisfies our aesthetic sense or our feeling for how things essentially are or ought to be. Interpretation is more specific in that certain actions are prescribed, certain words clearly adapted to the occasion, certain concepts formed and clearly articulated — all of which satisfies our reason and intellect. Analysis-clarification is still more specific in that concepts, words and actions are more clearly, more intricately defined, which also satisfies intellect-reason.

Communication: Planned-Adaptive, Subtle-Reflective, Definition-Study. Communication is one of the special domains of the third ray, although all types communicate. The most basic element of communication is the word. Facility with words, either spoken or written, is enhanced, generally speaking, when the third ray conditions either the soul, personality or mental body. In an unbalanced or pronounced condition the third ray influence can lead to too many words, talking too much, and a long and involved writing style. In proper balance it can lead to the right use of the appropriate word. One of the key words describing the third ray is *adaptability*. The right and appropriate word is the word that has been *adapted* to the circumstance. The word that properly *interprets* the thought is the word that has been *adapted* to the circumstance. The right, appropriate, properly adapted word results in *communication*, which in turn brings about new intellectual and physical activity.

K.T. Hostiuk in his book *Contemporary Organization* defines communication in the following way: "The whole purpose of communication in the organization is to bring about some desired action on the part of the receiver. To do this, the need for information transmittal must be recognized, the thought must be complete, and it must be relevant. . . . The managerial functions of planning and controlling . . . rely heavily on communication."[9] Communication is related to intelligent "planning." It deals with bringing about some "desired action." The thought must be "complete," that is, it must be *intelligent* or well thought-out. It must also be 'relavant," that is, appropriately *adapted* to the situation at hand.

This may become clearer if contrasted to communication styles of the fifth and fourth ray types. The fifth ray type, being analytical and interested in the clarity of precision, is much slower to communicate and less adaptable than the third ray type. The pronounced fifth ray type speaks from the point of view of a body of knowledge that rests on *clear definitions*. Being the expert, he is a good person to consult, but he is less adaptable to the great variety of circumstances than is the more eclectic third ray type. His speech tends to be slow, cautious and thoughtful. The speech of the third ray type tends to be quick and surprisingly appropriate for all its quickness.

The third and fifth rays working in combination are said to lead to the "master of the pen." Consider the following passage from *Esoteric Psychology:* "The third and the fifth rays make the perfectly balanced historian who grasps his subject in a large way and verifies every detail with patient accuracy. . . . The literary style of the third ray man is too often vague and involved, but if influenced by the first, fourth, fifth or seventh rays, this is changed, and under the fifth he will be a master of the pen."[10] It is interesting to note that the combination of three and five work well in the field of history. The third ray enables the historian to "grasp his subject in a large way", and the fifth ray enables him to "verify every detail with patient accuracy." History is not science. The Greek historian Pausanias, second century after Christ, wrote ten books on his travels through the Peloponnesus, Rome, Syria, and

Palestine. He *simply describes* temples, theatres, tombs, statues, pictures, monuments of every sort. He also mentions mountains, rivers and fountains, and mythological tales. History needs to be *interpreted*. The selection of certain events over others is in itself interpretation. Pausanias had the scientific attitude of wanting to describe, without interpretation, everything he saw.

Technical writing is a good example of the fifth ray style of communication. It is well-defined and clear but difficult to understand. That is, it is clear to those who already know, who are themselves experts in the field, but tends not to adapt itself to, say, a more general audience. Being scientific it must necessarily be accurate and precise. Where *adaptation* is involved, there is going to be some loss of accuracy. Where expediency is involved, there is going to be some loss of precision. Therefore, more of a burden is placed on the audience or upon those who desire to know or who want to be able to operate the particular mechanism. The burden is that they themselves must take the time and effort to learn the definitions and principles upon which the body of knowledge is built. They themselves must study and analyze. So, unlike the third ray, which has uncanny skill at adapting itself immediately (actively) to any particular situation, the fifth ray communication requires time and study. The fifth ray type is less intelligently active than the third ray type, but more analytically studious. The scope of the third ray tends to be a broad one, but accuracy may be sacrificed. The scope of the fifth ray type will tend to be narrower and accuracy will be a major priority.

The fourth ray type communicates in yet another mode. In *Esoteric Psychology* it is stated that the fourth ray type "will generally talk well and have a sense of humour, but he varies between brilliant conversations and gloomy silences, according to his mood."[11] This is very unlike the fifth ray type for several reasons: The fifth ray type achieves a mental focus with greater facility and, therefore, is not subjected to the swing of emotional mood nearly as much as the fourth ray type, generally speaking. Secondly, the fifth ray type can be quite comfortably silent, assuming the attitude of the detached observer, and therefore tends not to project any emotional gloom. Thirdly, the fifth ray type is not the brilliant conversationalist, for the scientific type defines rather than entertains, clarifies rather than dramatizes. The *third ray type* may not achieve those levels of brilliant conversations, but he will, generally speaking, be a far more consistent good conversationalist than the fourth ray type. This is due in part to the fact that the third ray type can *intelligently adapt* to most any situation.

The fourth ray effort to *reveal the inner meaning* is far less *adaptable* than is the *planned, intelligent activity* of the third ray type. Therefore, the "lines of communication", one could say, are far more tenuous, far more conditional, in the case of the fourth ray type than in that of the third ray. Revelation, as mentioned, has been defined as an "enlightening or astonishing disclosure." Revelation is, indeed, enlightening, astonishing, a matter of brilliance and related to the intuition. As a factor of the intuition, it is far rarer than a developed intellect. The fourth ray type, in order to reveal the brilliance of the inner meaning, must painstakingly try to cultivate those conditions within himself (and within a group) that will bring about the tenuous alignment. But communication is a two-way flow. A brilliant soliloquy is not communication. A demonstration of brilliance can easily turn into an object of ridicule. The outer conditions, the conditions of the situation and the people present, must also be "right" in order for the two-way flow of energy, the communication, to occur. Who could reveal more brilliance than Christ? And yet He Himself was not able to preach or teach "in his own country, and in his own house," for the people said: "Is not this the carpenter's son" and "they were offended in him."[12] This is rather an extreme analogy, but the point is, the brilliance of the revelation of the inner meaning is not easily and readily adaptable to outer conditions. Under just the right conditions a brilliant conversation can occur. Under just the right conditions an experience edifying to all can come about. In other words, communication as a work of art is a delicate matter, indeed. Communication as a factor of intelligence is less delicate, more adaptable, and also can be more forceful. The following passage from Maurice Nicoll's *The New Man* illustrates the struggle that the fourth ray type tends to have with the factor of communication:

> Higher knowledge, higher meaning, if it falls on the ordinary level of understanding, will either seem nonsense, or it will be wrongly understood. It will then become useless, and worse. Higher meaning can only be given to those who are close to grasping it rightly. This is one reason why all sacred writings — that is, writings that are designed to convey more than the literal sense of the words — must be concealed, as it were, by an outer wrapping. It is not a question of misleading people, but a question of

preventing this higher meaning from falling in the wrong place, on lower meaning, and thereby having its finer significance destroyed. People sometimes imagine they can understand anything, once they are told it. But this is quite wrong. The development of the understanding, the seeing of differences, is a long process. Everyone knows that little children cannot be taught about life directly because they are small. Again, it is realised that there are subjects in ordinary life that cannot be understood save by long preparation, such as certain branches of the sciences. It is not enough to be merely told what they are about.[13]

There are certain similarities here between the fourth and fifth rays. In order for a fifth ray type of communication to occur, the individual must bring some study and analytically clear thought of his own to the occasion. Similarly, in order for a person to appreciate a work of art, one must bring a fine sensitivity that attunes to the inner and hidden meaning. But then it is only still later when the person *reflects* on the inner meaning that the communication occurs. The work of art, the brilliant conversation, refers not to something that can be put into words and clarified, but to something that can only be implied and alluded to. And to get at that subtlety, one reflects long after the curtain has descended and long after the book or the conversation has been closed. The communication of the third ray type may also give one much food for reflection, but the reflection on the subtle meaning is not at the heart of third ray communication. With the fourth ray method communication may or may not come about. With the third ray energy, communication, indeed, must come about. So with the third ray we are dealing not so much with subtle nuances of meaning as with the "clear pronouncing of the truth."[14] While the fourth ray type may have a disdain for the lack of vision or the lack of deeper meaning in a given situation or field of endeavor, the third ray type will *adapt* its truth in such a way that it will bring about change or an *activity* that expresses greater *intelligence*. The fourth ray type, then, will certainly have more difficulty communicating than will the third ray type. The fourth ray type, however, very much wants to communicate, very much wants to generate and experience that *harmony* of good communication; but, being the Ray of Harmony through Conflict, there may also be present conflict and "gloomy silences."

The Case of a Third Ray Soul. We'll call him Matthew. After closely observing him at his place of employment for over a year, I came to the conclusion that he has the following ray equipment:

Soul   Mind 1

III   Personality 6   Emotion 6

                             Physical 1 or 3

First of all, it is readily observable that Matthew is very *active* both *physically* and *verbally*. In his late fifties, he is actually more active than many people half his age. He has a spritely, quick demeanor, always ready to get up and get whatever is needed or to undertake some immediate and necessary action. Lazyness and lethargy are the antithesis of this alert and energized person. As well as being active in the quantitative sense of doing a lot of things and being visibly a very busy person, qualitatively one could say that the activity is marked by *intelligence*. In other words, there is an efficiency to his activity, which suggests careful planning, consulting others, and learning from past experience. There is not evidenced a helter-skelter activity, a mere busyness, without thought or design (although the presence of helter-skelter activity in others could very well indicate the possibility of the third ray conditioning one of the vehicles). There is an alert concentration brought to most all of his activity.

Verbally he is noticeably also very active. He is, in fact, one of the most loquacious persons that I personally have ever met. He has a completed point of view on a great variety of subjects and is generally quick to express it. In this regard he is distinctly unlike those types who listen long and carefully, and who are very reluctant to express an opinion. Whatever matter comes up, he is sure to have a ready anecdote or a clearly thought-out statement to underscore a particular principle. Speaking is truly one of his special gifts. He is never at a loss for words, and his words are generally appropriate, diplomatic, clear and intelligent. To most of us, words come with difficulty. As we speak, there is often hesitation, doubt, reluctance on the one hand or too much chattering and thoughtlessness on the other. With Matthew facile and appropriate speech seems to come with remarkable ease.

The qualitatively descriptive phrase "the clear pronouncing of the truth" is one that D.K. uses in connection with the third ray.[15] Perhaps it may be of help if we once again contrast this factor with rays four and five. The fourth ray type, as mentioned, often has difficulty with such factors as clarity, accuracy, precision and adaptability. The fourth ray type generally relies more on suggestion, analogy, subtle innuendo, implication, colorful rather than clear speech, and often on exaggeration in order to dramatize a point. The fifth ray type tends to make clear statements, but with the pronounced fifth ray type these statements tend to be cautiously conservative, more indicative of verifiable knowledge than philosophical truth. Even when the fifth ray type moves into philosophical areas, which it is certainly capable of doing, there is a marked difference between the third and fifth ray types. The two phrases — the *clear* pronouncing of the truth (3) and *the clear statement of knowledge* (5) — can help to typify this difference if we consider them in the esoteric sense of designating different energies. The *pronouncing of truth* has more of a commanding, gripping, or arresting quality. It is something used in the midst of some action and it is something that tends to affect immediately the course of events. (One can see how the first and third rays working together are a powerful combination in governing and in business.) The *statement of knowledge* is more for our reflection, our consideration. It is more of an isolated piece of information, more technical, less adaptive. The fifth ray energy seems to affect the intellect in a more isolated and often very refined fashion, whereas the third ray, although affecting intellect, also brings in something of the will and affects the plane of activity as well.

Matthew, then, with a third ray soul and a first ray mind is verbally very effective. There is a certain power to his words, a certain control of situations through his intelligently clear yet quick words. These words might indicate a well thought-out way for doing things. While others may be wondering just exactly what is the truth in the matter, Matthew will quickly make a *clear pronouncement of truth* that is very difficult to argue with. Philosophically, of course, one could argue with anything, but in the context of the immediate situation, his statements of truth tend to be most appropriate, most adaptive.

From a philosophical point of view one might have a little difficulty with the word "truth." In other words, some ask "What is truth?" in the absolute sense. If something is this way today and that way tomorrow, then how can we say that there is a true way? If different viewpoints give different yet reasonable opinions, how can we say where the truth of the matter lies? The very nature of truth, however, is that it is adaptable to the situation at hand. To take any particular case or situation or act or principle and try to fix it in the absolute is the antithesis of truth. That something is this way today and that way tomorrow does not negate that there is such a thing as truth, rather it testifies to the *adaptibility of* truth. As opinions differ, some may approximate truth, others may be reasonable but untrue, still others might be a "clear pronouncing of the truth." Truth is adaptable, but that does not mean that truth compromises and becomes half-truth. Truth is adaptable, but that does not mean that it is arbitrary and therefore equal with untruth. The adaptability of truth is such that there is no situation (absolutely no situation) in which truth cannot find its expression, its manifestation, its evolution, its act, *its word.* Those who are conditioned by the third ray have then the gift and the possibility of clearly pronouncing the truth and acting intelligently in any given situation.

Some words go to the heart. Some words are colorful and beautiful. Some words are dramatic over-statements. Some words indicate the factor of power. Some words are wise. Some words indicate the form. And some words are a clear pronouncing of the truth. Matthew could both indicate the power factor and pronounce the truth with remarkable facility. His words, however, were not always wise. Wisdom uses fewer words, relies more on silence, and tends to look at the larger picture. Wisdom may lack the quick response needed in the emergency or crucial situation. Wisdom (second ray) likes to brood but is reluctant to act. Intelligent Activity (third ray) rules, one might say, where immediate action is required — and such is Matthew's occupational situation.

Another remarkable third ray quality that Matthew demonstrates is the *ability to formulate a clear plan of action.* (In *Esoteric Psychology*, II, "the urge to formulate a plan" is given as the third factor or Rule for Inducing Soul Control.) This requires intelligence, adaptability, the ability to communicate, and the ability to look at the immediate future and the short term necessities. An analogy he gave at one time (and he is not particularly good at finding the right analogy) to illustrate the intelligence of avoiding the pending crisis was simply: If you're riding a horse down a road and you see someone ahead taking out the garbage, you temporarily avoid passing that way, for clanging garbage cans can "spook" a horse. One has to determine the immediate possibilities, and then one has to formulate a specific plan that will avoid or meet the pending situation. One does not approach the situation with some *mystical hope* that everything will turn out for the best as some fourth ray and sixth ray types are likely to do. Also one does not simply sit back in a *detached* fashion and *observe* matters, as some fifth ray types may appropriately or inappropriately do. Rather one thinks intelligently, assessing the problem and taking action to avoid, mitigate or solve the problem.

Due to the fact that there is a three-one combination here (third ray soul and first ray mind), the ability to formulate a plan in a practical and realisitic fashion was evidenced. A third ray type without the practical grounding of a first or seventh ray influence could become the impractical activist who busies himself with many projects but doesn't actually get much done. Or he could be the planner, the schemer, the one who comes up with intricate and complex plans that never get off the ground and never seem to work.

The third ray is an important ray in the "field of business", and in the "handling of money." It deals with "concretized energy" which "we call money" and may negatively express itself as "pure materialism."[16] There is a book entitled *The Young Man in Business* by Howard Lee Davis which is a dated and somewhat curious little volume but of interest to us in its clear statement of certain basic premises. "Business," he writes, "is constantly looking for those who have common sense, native intelligence, the ability to reason clearly to the best solution of a problem, the vision to forsee the probable and the possible results of any proposed action, and the ability to work and get along well with other people, regardless of where they obtained their educations."[17] Thus, he emphasizes "intelligence", "reason", planning ("vision to forsee") and adaptability in the area of human relations — very distinctly third ray qualities in their esoteric sense, but also qualities that would seem to fit just about every walk of life if considered more generally in the exoteric sense. He goes on to say: "It is also necessary for a man to be able to express himself clearly in speech and in writing. A man may have reasoned out the best possible solution to a given problem, but of what value is that plan if he cannot impart it clearly and with conviction to his business associates as well as to those with whom he desires to do business?"[18] Expressing oneself clearly in speech is a prelude to the "clear pronouncing of the truth." It is a quality generally not necessary in most of the arts and in most facets of the sciences. It is, however, most helpful in government and generally most necessary in business.

Planning is another factor that H.L. Davis emphasizes: "It is essential for a man to plan so that he may be able to handle readily and efficiently the unusual situations that arise. The ability to do this will come if a man plans to be: intelligent in the handling of his work; accurate in all he does; as speedy as he can be without neglecting accuracy and the intelligent consideration of his problems. By having a workable plan, it should never be necessary to shoot until he has a good view of the target. He may not make a bull's eye every time, but at least he will see his objective clearly and aim for it."[19] We see here several third ray qualities in this summary statement by a man who has devoted his life to business and to the training of others for the world of business. *Planning* and *efficiency* are emphasized. "Intelligent in the handling of his work" is another way of saying *intelligent activity*. Speed without neglecting accuracy and intelligence is another way of saying *efficiency* or *economy*. The analogy of the bull's eye is interesting in that he is saying, you don't have to be perfectly accurate, you don't have to have the precision of, say, a scientist, but you do have to know what you're aiming for and you have to be on target. Speed and accuracy are very important, generally speaking, in the business world. But precision is necessary in the scientific world, and for that you sacrifice speed. Elsewhere he writes: "He should get facts — real facts! A man should be ready for, and receptive to, new facts that may justify a change of plan, but he should not move blindly on impulse."[20] The fourth ray type may appear to move more frequently "blindly on impulse." An everyday example of this would be impulsive buying. The fourth ray type may tend to have a greater inclination to buy something impulsively, not knowing whether or not the price is a good one and not comparing competitive products. The third ray type would consider such a method to be very foolish. The third ray type would take the effort to know the product and know whether it is a good price or not. And he would often manipulate matters in such a way as to get the best possible price. The third ray approach would be the more *intelligent* approach. The fourth ray type, however, could be more sensitive to the fact that the *right* object, the thing that perfectly meets the real need, has a way of "falling into one's lap" or "crossing one's path" is such a way that it far surpasses our most analytically intelligent approach. To some this appears "impulsive", but it is more akin to the *intuition*. Thus, the third ray type would tend to approach such matters analytically and with careful planning, that is, intelligently. The fourth ray type, as a path of least resistance, would tend to approach such matters either impulsively (emotionally) or intuitively.

My observation of Matthew is that he always uses an intelligent, analytical approach to buying, and that he never buys anything impulsively. He is exceptionally keen in this matter of making a purchase. His path of least resistance is, indeed, to think and scrutinize the matter from many angles. He has many a story to tell about how he got a good quality item at a special price. There was a particular publication of a series of training courses for eighty-three dollars advertised in a trade publication. It was just what he wanted. But he waited. Some months later there was an over-stock sale that reduced the price 25%. Still he waited. Then there was the damaged-in-freight sale, which reduced it more than 50%, followed by yet two more sales. He finally purchased the item for nine dollars. Not all items will go that distance, but he had a good sense of what items would.

When Matthew planned a trip to Europe, he planned almost everything in advance down to a very fine detail. He literally knew where every penny was to be spent. He got quality accommodations at a very reasaonable price; every step of the way was carefully prearranged. Some types tend not to plan at all. When traveling, they prefer to let the journey unfold before them, unplanned and full of surprises (and surprising hardships as well). Some types plan in a vague and general way. Many people plan only that which necessitates planning and remain vague and general on other matters. Still others plan just about everything and many things in great detail. Such a pronounced type is Matthew. Administrative work in business and government, in which planning is so necessary, is the general area of his experience and knowledge.

On the negative side, Matthew's sixth ray personality along with the first ray mind and third ray soul can bring about at times an almost fanatical persistence to an idea or plan of action, fortified by a battery of well-articulated phrases. Once having thought a matter through, tenacious adherence to a point can eclipse clear reason. The combination of rays one and six can be a difficult one to work with and integrate. A fanatical belief plus a driving will can wreak havoc when one loses sight of the whole picture, relatively speaking. Matthew is, however, developed enough for his eclectic, intelligent and adaptive soul to be brought into play, to shed light on every issue, and to loosen any excessive tenaciousness. Since the primary focus of consciousness is in the mind-personality, it may take some time for the soul influence to come about. The personality tends to make its mistakes first, and then quiet reflection days, months or years later may bring about soul illumination.

In Summation: First of all there is the *energy* factor. The third ray type has an abundance of it, and this may express itself as physical or intellectual activity. He may appear to be constantly "on the go", urging others to greater activity, or he may be occupied with a very complex and intricately involved intellectual study of some sort or another. There is also the factor of *economy* and *efficiency*. Although with some types there can be too much activity to the point of inefficiency, nevertheless, efficiency is one of the desired goals of the third ray type. Indeed, many third ray types accomplish much because there are efficient. Business, generally influenced by the third ray, epitomizes the need for and expression of efficient, economic activity. *The clear pronouncing of the truth* is another important factor in respect to the third ray. Where others hesitate with cautious reserve and still others rely on implication and vague innuendo, the third ray type has a special ability to adapt to and affect the immediate course of events through the clear pronouncing of the truth. Negatively, this can lead also to a special ability to manipulate others through false speech that rings true. Another important third ray factor deals with the ability to *formulate a clear plan of action*. Efficiency is not possible without a plan. To plan requires intelligence and careful thought. "Playing things by ear" as you go along requires sensitivity but can result in moving blindly on impulse. Planning relates one more directly to the factor of will, to the factor of intelligence or mind, and to the physical plane.

The Case of a Third Ray Mind. Mark has a second ray soul, fourth (or possibly sixth) ray personality, third ray mind, sixth ray emotional body and third ray physical body. The most striking difference to be noted is that in the case of Matthew there is a predominance of the 1-3-5-7 line of energy, balanced by a sixth ray personality and emotional body. In the case of Mark there is a predominance of the 2-4-6 line of energy balanced by a third ray mind and physical nature. Thus, in Matthew's case: III 6 161. In Mark's case: II 4 363. They have the sixth ray and the third ray in common.

What differences and what similarities would one expect to find in these two individuals in respect to the third ray? One of the "vices" of the second ray is "over-absorption in study." Thus, a second ray soul and a third ray mind might very well tend to bring about a state of *intellectual activity* rather than intelligent activity, that is, an activity of the intellect rather than physical plane activity. And such is the case. Mark is not a particularly handy person, whereas Matthew is. Mark knows little more about auto repair than changing a tire, whereas Matthew knows a considerable amount. In many incidences Mark will be the "bungler" or the person with "all thumbs" when it comes to physical plane work, whereas Matthew plans and carries out physical plane projects with care, skill, accuracy and completeness. Mark is not particularly neat or organized. Things pile up on his desk, books are stacked in odd places, notes and papers are scattered here and there — until one fine day it becomes so intolerably disorganized that he moves through his study busily and energetically straightening out and organizing everything in a flurry of activity. Matthew, on the other hand, is exceptionally orderly and well-organized. His house is spotless, everything in its place. He is very neat at all times. He knows exactly where to find some tool or some carefully filed document. When it comes to more purely intellectual activity the picture changes. Mark has considerably more academic training than Matthew. Mark loves the area of psychology in particular but is well-read in a broad and synthesized field of psychology-religion-philosophy-education, whereas Matthew has practical skill in the areas of business and administrative work. Mark reads almost every spare minute he has. He listens to tapes of books on his way to work. Matthew, on the other hand, reads only occasionally and then frequently on practical matters or "how-to-do-something" type of book.

Although in Mark's case there is *intellectual* activity and in Matthew's case intelligent *activity*, the significant factor is that, when compared to others, they are both extra-ordinarily active. Side by side with his work colleagues, whether in a business setting or in a social service agency, Matthew does much more work, if not twice as much, as his associates. That work can be both administrative and physical. Mark, in association with those of like intellectual interest, similarly stands out as the most intellectually active one. He reads more, studies more, writes more, compiles more information of a scholarly nature than do his fellow researchers and scholars.

Another significant similarity is verbal activity and communication. Both Mark and Matthew are verbally active. They stand out among others as being loquacious and articulate. They are never at a loss for words and they don't like silence. Mark, as well as Matthew, has a certain ability to "clearly pronounce the truth" within his own field of knowledge and interest. This is to say that his words can be both *adaptive* to the immediate situation at hand, and they are also *arresting* in that the cutting edge of truth startles one into a more insightful way of seeing the particular issue at hand. Wisdom, in contrast, is generally not so arresting, requires more brooding and reflecting to understand it, and can be but a hint or suggestion that easily passes over the head of the intended recipient. Also to draw forth wisdom (second ray) one must inquire, whereas truth (third ray) can more actively jump in and impose itself on the situation.

In *Esoteric Psychology* we read: "The servers on this ray have a special function at this time in stimulating the intellect of humanity, sharpening it and inspiring it. They work, manipulating ideas so as to make them more easy of comprehension by the mass of intelligent men and women. . . . Ideas . . . are adapted to the immediate need and rendered vocal by the force of the intellectual third ray types."[21] Both Matthew and Mark are able to "*adapt ideas to the immediate need and render them vocal,*" thus *stimulating the intellect* of those in their sphere of influence. In Matthew's case the intellect is stimulated in such a way that one tends to deal with physical and power issues in a more refined and intelligent manner. In Mark's case the intellect is stimulated in such a way that one deals with psychological issues in a more refined and intelligent manner. When it comes to spiritual-religious questions Mark's understanding far surpasses that of Matthew. With a second ray soul this would be expected. Both Mark and Matthew share one of the "vices" of the third ray type, that of "*jumping from point to point.*" The point, instead of being a relevant factor of truth, can be irrelevant, extraneous or only a loosely related factor. Mark is more susceptibile to this activity of jumping from point to point due probably to the two-three ray combination. The abstract second ray is a broadening and expansive influence. It would like to include everything. Matthew, on the other hand, with a three-one combination struggles more successfully to bring this under control. In any matter of any importance or significance, the first ray deals in a concentrated fashion with the immediate problem at hand. In a crisis situation one simply cannot jump from point to point. During casual conversations, however, Matthew too would go very rapidly from point to point. Looking at anything from a peripheral or form or activity angle, there are indeed so many points that one could make. One's speech becomes hurried in order to get in as many points as possible.

In Mark's case the third ray is more likely to provide a *negative* factor than in Matthew's case for the following reasons: Mark *has* a developed intellect. His concrete mind is not in the process of developing as much as it is already developed. It is necessary for him to go on to the next unit of consciousness, that of integrating the threefold personality and developing soul consciousness, which he is in the process of doing. From a ray point of view, the second ray then is of paramount importance to him. Less intellectualism and learning how to "think in the heart" instead of thinking in the "throat center", that is, instead of thinking with a torrent of words, would be of benefit to him. In *Esoteric Psychology* certain aphoristic statements are given as "ray techniques imposed by the soul upon the personality after it has been somewhat integrated into a functioning unity."[22] For the third ray the technique includes the statement: "Be still. Learn to stand silent quiet and unafraid. . . . Rush not from point to point, nor be deluded by the outer forms and that which disappears." Although we are speaking about the third ray at the level of the mental unit, it seems to me that some of the aphoristic statements could be well applied to Mark. There is the need to guard against over-stimulation (over-activity) of the intellect, the need to prevent the rushing from point to point, the need for intellectual stillness.

In Matthew's case the third ray is more likely to provide a *positive* factor for the following reasons: "The method of approaching the great Quest, for this ray type, is by deep thinking on philosophic or metaphysical lines till he is led to the realisation of the great Beyond and of the paramount importance of treading the Path that leads thither."[23] Matthew needs to think more deeply on philosophical and metaphysical matters. (Mark already thinks very deeply on these matters.) Matthew's first ray mind directions his thought along physical rather than metaphysical lines. This aspect of his psychological equipment is already developed and refined. Also, as mentioned, Matthew's one-six ray combination can bring about at times an excessively tenacious almost fanatical adherence to a particular metaphysical, moral or religious point of no great profundity. There is the need to think much more deeply along the more abstract philosophical line of thought.

Misuse of Third Ray Energy: Selfish Manipulation, the False Word, Rushing From Point to Point. It is mentioned in *Esoteric Psychology* that, on the positive side, the third ray energy can lead to "manipulating ideas so as to make them more easy of comprehension",[24] and to "the manipulation of energy in order to reveal beauty and truth."[25] On the negative side the third ray energy can lead to "force manipulation through selfish desire",[26] a tendency to "manipulate forces and energies and to "pull strings" in order to bring about desired ends",[27] and a tendency to be a "scheming manipulator or a fighter for immense schemes which can never really materialize."[28] Obviously the word "manipulation" is in some way especially descriptive of the third ray, and, therefore, we ought to endeavor to ascertain its esoteric sense as best we can.

To "manipulate" originally meant "to grip or clasp with the hands, also to reduce into bottles or handfuls, to bundle up" (Oxford English Dictionary). Thus, manipulation is related to the hands. The hands deal with the *activity* aspect in that our most refined physical activity engages the use of the hands. The hands are used in carrying or transporting an object from one room to another, one location to another. The hands are used in *fashioning* and *manipulating* an instrument or weapon. Considering the subtler body of the mind, *words* become the key agent of manipulation. We manipulate others for good or ill (direct, influence, organize, handle, manage, utilize, control) to a great extent *through the use of words*. On a higher turn of the spiral it would be the spiritual will (atma) by means of which others can be manipulated (directed and influenced); but this occurs, it seems to me, only when the personality is itself being directed by the spiritual will where the illusion of separativeness and therefore selfish manipulation is no longer a possibility. So we have the *hands*, the *word* and the *will* through which manipulation occurs. One could say that the *first* aspect of third ray manipulation deals with the will and affects *being*. The *second* aspect of third ray manipulation deals with the *word* and affects *consciousness*. And the *third* aspect of third ray manipulation deals with the *hands* and affects *physical* plane objects.

On the physical plane a third ray influence would lead to such conditions as coordination, dexterity, a robust and energized constitution, an activeness, an industriousness, a facility, etc. When the plane of the intellect is brought into play, then we have manipulation through words, communication, planning, which negatively becomes cunning, conning, scheming, the use of intrigue, "pulling strings", craftiness, etc. In one instance the individual is making clear statements of truth adapted to the situation at hand, and in another instance the individual is most cleverly concealing the truth — and on the surface of things many times it is very difficult to distinguish between the two. Just as the third ray type has a special skill, a special *power*, with the right use of the true word, so also the third ray type has a special skill at *making the false word appear true*. The fourth ray type, in contrast, is concerned with the *revelation of meaning*, which negatively becomes *veiling* meaning and thus generating *glamours*. The generation of glamours has a general, pervasive effect on consciousness. The third ray type, in contrast to the cloudy, pervasive effect of the fourth ray type, has something more specific in mind. He wants you to believe that a specific something is true — though he knows it is not — in order that a specific activity, a specific act, is brought about. Thus the words "cunning, conning, scheming" are more apt. Since the third ray type has a special gift with words (being able to use words in an effective, adaptive way and also being able to recognize in a special way the power of the true word), it also follows that the special gift can be selfishly misused and the third ray type can be a great con-artist.

The word *true* stems from *(ge)triewe* (Old English), *truwe* (Middle English), and *triuwa* (Old High German), meaning "having or characterized by good faith, covenant." *Truth* etymologically is related to *troth*, "honesty, making a solemn promise or engagement," and *truce*, "fidelity to a promise, assurance of faith, truth, promise, covenant."[29] Thus, if we think of "speaking truth" in its legal and business sense — the sense of a "covenant", a "solemn promise", that is, a verbal contract, a promise to deliver certain goods or perform certain actions — then we may approach closer to the special use or misuse of the energy of the word available to the third ray type. As the fourth ray is an important factor in the world of culture and the arts, and the fifth ray an important factor in the world of science, so the third ray is an important factor in the world of business (as well as philosophy). Indeed, where is there more *activity*, necessarily of an *intelligent* nature (though not necessarily wise) than in the world of business. And where is the *truthful word*, in the sense of covenant, promise, contract, of greater importance on a day to day basis than in the world of business. But one might also say, where is there a greater misuse of words and where are there greater "con-artists" or the *scheming manipulators* than in the world of business. Thus, the third ray type often has a special gift at stimulating the intellect of others so that others see the truth in any given situation, or they can misuse that gift and manipulate others, through a clever deceptive use of the word, for their own personal advantage.

Another misuse of the energy of the third ray is the *rushing from point to point*. This is in a sense simply too much activity. On the physical plane it can be a rushing from activity to activity, project to project — a busy-ness. On the mental plane it can be a rushing from intellectual point to intellectual point. I recently attended a workshop where the facilitator had, indeed, a lot of material to cover and a great many points to make. The words came out so fast that they sort of tumbled over each other. The way the lecturer characterized it was that he felt that he was a "45 rpm record in a 33 1/3 world." At some level (mind, personality or soul) the third ray was present in the individual, though at what level it is difficult for me to say after one brief encounter. The lecturer rushed from point to point, many of which were intellectually stimulating and interesting, but there was a lack of a more precisely detailed scrutiny and study indicative of the fifth ray type. There was also a lack of that sensitive delivery that wants to turn a lecture into a work of art, which is more indicative of the fourth ray type.

Rushing from point to point generates the illusion of getting things done, the illusion of accomplishment. The fourth ray type tends to be more emotionally oriented and sensitive than the physically and intellectually oriented third ray type (though this could vary due to astrological influences and other ray factors). The fourth ray type runs the risk in wasting time in mood and, therefore, not accomplishing much, as the third ray wastes time in activity. The quiet, meditative, creative, reflective experience of the fourth ray type appears outwardly to be mood, but is in fact highly productive, or of special accomplishment that will lead to outer productivity. Negatively, however, the fourth ray type can be a creature of mood and, indeed, accomplish very little. An interesting distinction here, however, is that the third ray type tends to appear to be accomplishing much in his swirl of activity whether or not he is in fact accomplishing much at all. And contrariwise, it often tends to appear that the fourth ray type is not accomplishing much whether or not he in fact is. This is simply to say that intellectual and physical activity tends to be more visible or more clearly demonstrative than sensitive and intuitive activity. Both the fourth and fifth ray types in their distinct forms are very unlike the rushing from point to point of the third ray type.

Summary. In summation we have made a list of the positive and negative characteristics that could be evidenced in the person influenced by the third ray.

Positive	Negative
intelligent activity	lack of stillness
energetic	over stimulation
industrious	constantly on the go
adaptation	
coordination, dexerity	
Law of Economy	lack of organization
manipulating matter	selfish manipulation
efficient	too much activity
utilitarian	impractical
skill in business	busy-ness
interpretation, explanation	rushing from point to point
stimulate intellect	intellectualism
render ideas vocal	
communication	
Clear pronouncing of truth	too many words
facility with words	too much talking
appropriate word	false word
formulate plan of action	scheming, pulling strings
planned activity	overly complex plans
philosophical studies	
wideview abstract questions	
higher mind	
eclectic	

Reference Notes to Essay on Third Ray

1. Alice Bailey, *A Treatise on Cosmic Fire* (New York: Lucis Publishing Co., 1925), pp. 214-220.

2. Alice Bailey, *Esoteric Psychology*, vol. I (New York: Lucis Publishing Co., 1936), p. 329.
3. "It was the recognition of that which induced me to give you the word "interpretation" as your most important keyword, for it would evoke in you qualities along the line of the third Ray of Active Intelligence, which is closely allied to your fifth ray personality." Alice Bailey, *Discipleship in the New Age*, vol. I (New York: Lucis Publishing Co., 1944), p. 448.
4. Alice Bailey, *Esoteric Psychology*, vol. II (New York: Lucis Publishing Co., 1942), p. 246.
5. Will Durant, *The Story of Philosophy* (New York: Simon and Schuster, 1926), p. 2.
6. Alice Bailey, *Esoteric Psychology*, I, p. 204.
7. Ibid., p. 163.
8. Alice Bailey, *Discipleship in the New Age*, I, p. 279.
9. K. T. Hostiuck, *Contemporary Organizations* (Morristown, New Jersey: General Learning Press, 1974), pp. 241, 238.
10. Alice Bailey, *Esoteric Psychology*, I, p. 205.
11. Ibid., p. 207.
12. Matthew 14: 54-58.
13. Maurice Nicoll, *The New Man* (Great Britain: Stuart & Richards, 1950, rpt. Penguin Books, 1972), p. 3.
14. Alice Bailey, *Esoteric Psychology*, II, p. 37.
15. Ibid., p. 37.
16. Alice Bailey, *Discipleship in the New Age*, I, 379, 402. Alice Bailey, *Esoteric Astrology*, p. 244. Alice Bailey, *Rays and Initiations*, p. 80.
17. Howard Lee Davis, *The Young Man in Business* (New York: John Wiley and Sons, Inc., 1931), p. 2.
18. Ibid., p. 6.
19. Ibid., p. 67.
20. Ibid., p. 65.
21. Bailey, *Esoteric Psychology*, vol. II, p. 142.
22. Ibid., p. 351.
23. Bailey, *Esoteric Psychology*, vol. I, p. 205.
24. Bailey, *Esoteric Psychology*, vol. II, p. 142.
25. Ibid., p. 40.
26. Ibid., p. 40.
27. Bailey, *Esoteric Psychology*, vol. I, p. 394.
28. Bailey, *Esoteric Psychology*, vol. II, p. 444.
29. Oxford English Dictionary, 1971.

FIRST RAY:
"FOR YOU, THERE MUST BE NOT A CIRCLE, BUT A LINE."

I had been meeting with a particular study group for approximately three years when on one occasion an emotional eruption occurred. The eruption came through me. I was quite upset, to say the least. The issue centered around what I considered to be attitudes of competition and an undercurrent of a power struggle. During subsequent weeks the matter preoccupied my mind to the point of interfering with my daily duties. One night before going to bed I put the request for clarification on this troubling issue to the soul or the inner side, and had the following dream.

> I was at a study-group meeting, and we were discussing the first ray. I brought up the point that a most important quality of the first ray is the quality of *destruction*. J. (who in my opinion has the greatest understanding of the first ray of any in the group and who may have a first ray soul) agreed that destruction was an important quality but said there was another word for it. The word he mentioned was something like "exetimer" — though that was not quite it. "I never heard that word before," I said. "Let's look it up in the dictionary."
>
> As I was getting up I noticed for the first time a person sitting next to me on my left. (This person was actually nobody in our present group.) The remarkable quality of this person was that he was very silent, yet strong and alert. One felt his presence. On hearing the other word for destruction, he nodded with clear comprehension. The slight nod itself was a sort of statement of power. One might say that on the issue of direction one looked to him — that is, one involuntarily and automatically was attracted to and therefore turned towards the focal point of power — and he nodded.
>
> I got up to fetch a dictionary. I walked out of the room, out of the building and around towards the left,

crossing a lawn and following a circular walkway.
This was apparently a university complex. It was a
bright, clear day. On the left hand side there emerged
a shadow-like figure. He was starting to move down
the inclined walkway with a fancy little two-step.
"Hold on," I said. "There's no need to walk like that.
You have to be careful." The incline of the walkway
increased. There was also some sand on it, which
made it very slippery. I demonstrated to the shadowy
figure how one could move a delicate step at a time
over the sandy walk in order to avoid a dangerous
slide. But then *I* began to slide. I could not prevent
myself from sliding in spite of the precaution. The
walkway curved and descended into a series of concrete steps. I slid down the steps, bouncing from one
to the other. With great care I was able to maintain
a precarious up-right position. With each step I was
threatened with an unpleasant, possibly dangerous
fall. I went into a building which seemed to be a huge
gymnasium. In the corner of the gym was a small
bookstore that was apparently going out of business,
since everything was greatly reduced in price and
very few items were left. Surprisingly, one or two
members of the group were already at the bookstore
when I arrived. How was that possible since I was the
first to leave the meeting in search of a dictionary and
since nobody passed me on the way? One member of
the group had purchased a book, on the cover of which
was a medieval woodcut design with a skull being
most prominent. It appeared to be an occult novel. We
wondered if this would address the problem and help
us to define the word related to "destruction." It was
apparently the best book available, and in any case
it was quite a bargain and worth purchasing at the
price. I scanned the remaining books but no other
suitable books were available. I then noticed another
member of the group, a new member, one who had
not been to the group and yet somehow a member of
the group. I put my left arm around him and greeted
him. He was the quiet and alert type, the type that
maintained a presence of mind rather than an

exuberance of feeling. He also seemed a low-profile
type an unglamorous type. There seemed nothing
particularly distinguishing about him.

In any kind of group endeavor there is the need for destruction
if the group is to grow, create, evolve, be of service, do work, change,
etc. If certain things are not destroyed, there is the threat of stagna-
tion, of being static, of crystallization, etc. Destroying something,
however, is not easy and in many ways it is a rather thankless
task. Perhaps the major reason why it is a difficult task is that
people get hurt. Their comfortable habits and their pocketbooks
get hurt on the physical plane; their feelings, attachments, personal
sensitivities, and their sense of self-esteem get hurt on the
emotional plane; and their ideas, concepts, and plans get hurt on
the mental plane. Their positions of power and influence become
affected.

The word "destroying", however, is such a harsh word. Much pain
is associated with it. There must be another word we could use.
Esoterically speaking, when we refer to a "word" we are in fact
refering to a particular energy. Therefore, when the question is
asked, "Is there another word", it is being suggested that we try
to determine whether or not there is another kind of energy or
another kind of force emanation that we could use. The non-existent
term "exetimer" suggests a couple of things. First of all it brings
to mind a number of words with the prefix "ex", such as execute,
exit, exterminate, expel, expose, etc. All these energies are in a
sense destructive energies. To execute in a sense is *to carry out
an order* or *to put to death in compliance with a legal sentence.* To
exit is *to remove* oneself. To exterminate is *to uproot* or *eradicate.*
To expel is *to drive away.* To expose is *to reveal.* Destroying, then,
is a fine art. In order to destroy, one must use just the right force.
The able destroyer is being very selective, very discriminative in
terms of what force he chooses to apply. Destruction in a sense can
be equated with a surgical operation where one wants to eliminate
the threatening element. One does not want to eliminate or kill
the patient. We often get the picture that destruction is eradicating
everything in one's path, and therefore we often fail to see that
destruction is a fine art which enables a continual rejuvenation
of the manifesting life to occur.

The prefix "ex" has the meaning of "out of", "from", "without",
"exclusion from", "deprived of" and "destitute of." "Ex" as a prefix
sometimes has the motion of away from oneself, in contrast to the

prefix "in" which has motion towards oneself. Thus, we have inhale and exhale, include and exclude, inhibit and exhibit, internalize and externalize, etc. It is interesting to note in this regard that of the seven laws of soul or group life (as given in *Esoteric Psychology*, II, pp. 85-200) the energy of the "law of repulse" is given as the "rejecting energy of the first ray." Thus, we have still other and more appropriate names (and energies) for the little understood first ray function of destroying. We have repulsing, rejecting, repudiating, refusing, dissipating and scattering.

The word "exetimer", however, is unknown to us. So we set out in search of this other word for destruction. I circle around to the left. The shadow prompts me to move in a fancy way. I reject this, however, and move very cautiously. Nevertheless, I go into a dangerous slide. I arrive at the destination or objective later than the others. A "technique of integration" for the first ray type includes the following: "The love of power must dominate. There must also be repudiation of those forms which wield no power. The word goes forth from soul to form; 'Stand up. Press outward into life. Achieve a goal. For you, there must be not a circle, but a line. Prepare the form.' " (*Eso. Psych.* II, pp. 351-2.)

For the *second ray type*, it seems to me, there tends to be *a circle*; for the *first ray type* there tends to be a *line*. The line goes directly to the point — the point of power, the point of form, the point of synthesis. In the dream I was *circling* around to my left. It was a beautiful, clear day. There was something enjoyable about the transition from one place to another. There was something enjoyable about the *longer way around*. But there was also something dangerous about it. The shadow prompted me to do a "fancy two step" or to a personal display of agility or talent — a sort of subtle something extra, a superfluous showing-off. From a first ray point of view it is a totally unnecessary diversion. It is not to the point. It does not move in a straight line. Every unnecessary step is simply increasing the possibility of getting tripped up.

I repudiate the shadow — the subtle personal display of agility — but I still prefer the longer way around. I am aware of the danger, and therefore I move with utmost caution. But still I slide. What is the circular way around, and what is the sliding? The slipping and sliding suggest the astral-emotional plane. The circular way suggests a way of wholeness. In contrast to the brevity and the to-the-point attitude of the first ray, the second ray is broad and expansive. It wants to include several points, several aspects, several planes of awareness, etc. The circular way is, in a sense, the *teaching* way. The teaching way deals more with consciousness than with power. "The sun is shining and it is a very clear day." The second ray likes to be *outside* — outside the building, outside the form. It likes to be under the expansiveness of the skies rather than the limitation of form. It is pleasant to go on circular diversions through the campuses of our endeavors. The circular diversions are enjoyable, entertaining, instructive, edifying — but they tend not to address specifically and directly the power issue of the particular synthesizing point. There is the tendency for the second ray type to include too much emotion in the power question or too much instruction. There is the tendency to play on one's sympathies, to make appeals to the finer sensitivities, to the sense of compassion, to the heart, etc. The first ray, on the other hand, cuts through the emotional factor, going in a straight line as it were, and "prepares the form."

We have here two distinctly different ways of viewing life and circumstances.

The First Ray	The Second Ray
The line.	The circle.
Directly to the point.	The long way around.
No emotion.	Including emotion.
Destroying old forms.	Reluctance to destroy, afraid of hurting.
Preparing the form.	Building within the prepared form.
Brevity of word.	Many words.
Taking action at point of power.	Teaching, addressing consciousness factor.
Straight line, looking neither to the right nor left.	Looking right, left, up and down, trying to include all aspects.

On the circular way, which includes the emotional, I begin to slide. No matter how cautious I am, no matter how I negate the frivolous little two-step, no matter how conscious I am of taking one careful step after the other — I still begin to slide or lose control. It is as if I am saying, "Okay now, I'm going to be extremely cautious as I move through the emotional plane." But there I am on the emotional plane and the nature of the emotional plane is such that it is slippery and one slides. The first ray type avoids the emotional factor altogether and goes directly — in a straight line — to the point. The point is a non-emotional point. This may cause emotions to rise in others but one does not allow oneself to be emotionally diverted from the issue. This does not mean that emotion does not have its rightful place in the general scheme of things, for it does. But the original question here concerns itself with a power struggle, *which is a first ray problem-situation,* and which can best be resolved by a first ray approach. The right use of this energy is what is lacking. The dream is indicating the inappropriateness of my present methods with the particular set of circumstances, i. e., the inappropriateness of a second ray energy to solve a first ray question.

Arriving at the bookstore, I am surprised to see that there are already one or two members of the group there. Nobody passed me on the way, so they must have gone a different route. One might say that they must have taken the less scenic but the more direct route, that is, the less enjoyable, less emotionally satisfying way. We are trying to define a word. The word is another word for destruction and has to do with the first ray. And the word designates a particular energy or force emanation. The processes that we are now undertaking — the non-emotional straight line, the alert presence, the silent nod, etc. — are in themselves the characterized or mythologized definition of this energy at one particular level. There is one pertinent book at the store and that is a book of fiction, occult fiction, with a skull on its cover. My reaction to both of these factors is a negative one. I never read occult fiction and I don't like death as symbolized by the skull. The indication seems to be, however, that I must try to do something that I don't particularly like to do. For purposes of wholeness, we are frequently prodded along unfamiliar and, therefore, difficult ways. In fiction we are not dealing with precise and scientific definitions. In the dream it is surprising to me that this book is the "best buy" there. The surprise element in the dream is the teaching element, the "new" idea. The surprise is the shock element needed to quicken greater consciousness. I was anticipating a dictionary or an occult glossary or some scholarly researched work. Why fiction? Fiction or literature suggests an involvement with rather than a detached observation or intellectualization of the particular subject matter. Literature is also a *creative* process. One must, it seems, deal with the matter of death or destruction not as something beyond our control or something that brings chaos in our lives, but as something that can be controlled and fashioned in a creative way. For the second ray type this is not a path of least resistance. The second ray type finds the task of destruction most unpalatable. In the dream this fact is brought home to me by my own recoiling from the skull figure. I do not like to destroy or eliminate, exclude or expel, expose, eradicate, etc. Nevertheless, the indication is that there is a need to be more involved in the creative use of the first ray energy that necessarily "destroys" — for lack of a milder or more innovatively appropriate term.

In the final gesture of the dream I put my left arm around a new group member, a member who in fact has not yet been to the group. He is quiet and alert. He maintains a presence of mind rather than an exuberance of feeling. He is a low-profile type. There seems nothing particularly distinguishing about him. The "new member" is, of course, a new aspect, a new energy, of myself. He is very ordinary and unthreatening in appearance and demeanor. There is a plainness, a certain lack of glamour, about the fellow. This is in contradistinction to many of the commonly held views on power and destruction. Many associate power with assertiveness, a domineering presence, ruthlessness, etc. Although this side of the power-destruction factor does exist, the less obvoius, less blatant, or less visible side is in fact the more powerful and more enduring side.

The dream then seems to be suggesting several things:

(1) First of all there is a need for the right use of first ray energy. The question of competition and power struggle indicates that we are dealing primarily with a first ray problem-situation and, therefore, first ray energy is needed to resolve the crisis.

(2) The second factor indicated is that, yes, destruction is a key factor, but we have to view this factor from an altogether different angle. It has to be defined in a much subtler, more refined way. Destruction is only used in an indiscriminant, broad-sweeping manner by the crude, by those unfamiliar with the energy, or by those inclined towards megalomania. Very careful discrimination is needed in order to apply this energy in an appropriate manner.

(3) The third point is that there is a mental-physical alignment necessary in order to effectively wield this energy. There is the necessity to go "straight to the point", to move in a straight line, by-passing the emotional nature. The circuitous path, exploring tangental matters and a sundry of personal feelings, in negated.

(4)   The fourth point is that this energy is used in a creative
         way. This ties in with the second point of refined defini-
         tion. Just the right aspect of this energy must be applied
         in just the right way. Right timing is involved here. Also
         there is the need to delicately remove just the cancerous
         element without doing damage to the surrounding tissue
         and adjacent organisms.

(5)   The fifth point is that one assumes a low-profile and not
         a leadership position. Paradoxically, in dealing with first
         ray issues, one ought not to assume an aggressive and
         pushy attitude. One ought not to try to make all the key
         decisions oneself. One ought not to impose one's will nor
         try to influence and control every course of action. The
         low-profile, unglamorous and undistinguishing
         demeanor suggests a non-self-aggrandizing position.
         Personal desire always draws something to the personal
         self. Here we have the need for a self-forgetful and
         selfless attitude. It is not personal power that is sought.
         One is alertly attuned to all power issues, but one does
         not seek one's personal will. Whose will is then being
         sought?

In quoting the "technique of integration" from *Esoteric
Psychology*, we ended with the sentences: "for you, there must be
not a circle, but a line. Prepare *the form*." The aphoristic statement continues:

> Let the eyes look forward, not on either side. Let the
> ears be closed to all the outer voices, and the hands
> clenched, the body braced, and mind alert. Emotion
> is not used in furthering of the Plan. Love takes its
> place. (*Eso. Psych.* II, p. 352)

There are two factors to be noted here: We are concerned with
the "furthering of the Plan." That would answer the question
"Whose will is it?" It is God's Will or God's Plan for Humanity.
We are dealing with spiritual principles and we are dealing with
archetypal patterns. There is a Plan, there is a right way, and we
are trying to determine what that way is in any given situation.
We are very much attuned to the unlikelihood that it is our way
or the way to which we have intellectually reasoned.

The second factor to be noted is that "emotion is not used" and
"love takes its place." Emotion interferes with the alert mind and
the mental-physical alignment. Emotion brings in an array of

personal sentiments and wishes that delay and confuse the need to take action in order to prepare the form. But love takes the place of emotion. Love does not interfere with the alert mind. On the contrary, it sharpens it. While emotion is personally sensitive, love is group conscious or conscious of the good of the whole. These two extra-personal or transpersonal factors (recognition of the Plan and attunement to group or soul love) guarantee, it seems to me, a safe and appropriate use of the first ray energy. As D.K. mentioned of the first ray type:

> Servers on this ray, if they are trained disciples, work through what might be called the imposition of the Will of God upon the minds of men. This they do through the powerful impact of ideas upon the minds of men, and the emphasis of the governing principles which must be assimilated by humanity. These ideas, when grasped by the aspirant bring about two developments. First, they initiate a period of destruction and of a breaking up of that which is old and hindering, and this is later followed by the clear shining forth of the new idea and its subsequent grasping by the minds of intelligent humanity. These ideas embody great principles, and constitute the New Age ideas. These servers, therefore, work as God's destroying angels, destroying the old forms, but nevertheless, behind it all lies the impetus of love. (*Esoteric Psychology*, vol. II. pp. 140-1.)

Glossary of Ray Definitions

The Seven Rays are "the seven breaths of the one Life . . ." producing "all states of consciousness in all fields of awareness." There is in fact "nothing in the whole solar system, at whatever stage of evolution it may stand, which does not belong and has not always belonged to one or other of the seven rays." "A ray is but a name for a particular force or type of energy, with the emphasis upon the quality which that force exhibits and not upon the form aspect which it creates." (*Esoteric Psychology,* I, pp. 44, 60, 163, 316.)

The First Ray of Power or Will. Souls on the power ray "are characterized by a dynamic will, and their power within the human family works out as the force of destruction that will produce liberation (*Eso. Psych.*, I, p. 63). The "revelation of power is obviously part of the expression of the first ray type" (*Eso. Psych,* II, p. 613). The first ray "to all intents and purposes is the energy of divine embodied will, which has been exoterically described as 'unavoidable directed purpose' " (*Eso. Astrology,* p. 195).

Some qualities, characteristics and factors of the first ray type (as seen in the human psychological condition) are: isolated independence, impersonality, courage, strength, fearlessness, power to govern, ambition and pride, organizing power, poise, administrative and managing skills, executive ability, logical tenacity, power to dynamically affect others, imposition of ideas, isolation and detachment, and an ability to force issues and determine results.

The Second Ray of Love-Wisdom is the "embodiment of pure love. This Life instills into all forms the quality of love, with its more material manifestation of desire, and is the attractive principle in nature and the custodian of the Law of Attraction" (*Eso. Psych,* I, p. 23). "This second ray is pre-eminently the ray of applied consciousness, and works through the creation and development of those forms which are found throughout the universe. They are essentially mechanisms for the development of responsiveness or awareness" (*Eso. Phych,* I, p. 45). Some qualitites, characteristics and factors associated with the second ray type are: patience, endurance, power to suffer and to agonize towards the goal, sensitivity, inclusiveness, honesty, intuition, calmness, serene temper, the gift of wise teaching, healing, understanding heart, overly attached to others, overly fearful or worrisome, and too rapid identification with others.

The Third Ray of Intelligent Activity "brings in the factor of discrimination through mental activity, and this, in its turn, balances the so-called love nature and it is in truth the cause of our evolutionary growth. The life in forms passes through discriminative and selective activity from one experience to another in an ever widening scale of contacts" (*Eso. Psych,* I, p. 338). The third ray is the "energy of intelligence, actively displayed in creative activity" (*Destiny of Nations,* p. 6). Adaptability is the "prime attribute ascribed to the Third Ray, or Brahma aspect. Therefore, fundamentally it may be considered as the attribute of intelligence which adapts the matter aspect to the Spirit aspect, and is a characteristic inherent in matter itself" (*Cosmic Fire,* p. 423).

Some qualities, characteristics and factors associated with the third ray are: clear intellect, articulate speech, eclecticism, adaptibility, tendency to formulate a plan, skill in handling money, manipulation, critical attitude, energy, over-active tendency, pride in intellect, and an ability to interpret or to render ideas so as to make them more easy of comprehension.

The Fourth Ray of Harmony Through Conflict, also called the **Ray of Harmony, Beauty and Art.** "The main function of this Being is the creation of Beauty (as an expression of truth) through the free interplay of life and form, basing the design of beauty upon the initial plan as it exists in the mind of the solar Logos" (*Eso. Psych.,* I, p. 24). The fourth ray "gives to all forms that which produces beauty and works towards the harmonizing of all effects emanating from the world of causes, which is the world of the three major rays" (*Eso. Psych.,* I, p. 49). "The result of this harmonizing activity is beauty, but it is a beauty that is achieved through struggle. This produces a livingness through death, a harmony through strife, a union through diversity and adversity" (*Eso. Psych.,* II, p. 92).

Some qualities, characteristics and factors associated with the fourth ray are: a sense of beauty, creativity, harmonizing, unifying, bridging, evocation of the intuition, the giving impulse, imagination, artistic impulse, strong affections, sympathy, exaggeration, inaccuracy, sense of color, sense of relationship, and a spirit of conflict in the cause of harmony.

The Fifth Ray of Scientific Knowledge "embodies the principle of knowledge and . . . has produced what we call science" (*Eso. Psych.*, I, p. 51). The fifth ray is "in reality, that on which a man learns to use all acquired knowledge of the 'form divine' in such a way that the inner life is served and the outer form becomes the magnetic expression of the divine life. It is the ray of intelligent love above all else, just as the second ray is the ray of intuitive love" (*Discipleship in the New Age*, I, p. 542).

Some qualities, characteristics and factors associated with the fifth ray are: exactitude, analysis, strictly accurate statements, sometimes a tendency to be pedantic, narrowness, mental separation, the true thinker or mental type, love of the form, power to discriminate, difficulty in seeing larger issue, and power to master chosen field of knowledge.

The Sixth Ray of Idealism and Devotion. "A militant focussing upon the ideal, a one-pointed devotion to the intent of the life urge, and a divine sincerity are the qualities of this Lord, and set their impress upon all that is found within His body of manifestation" (*Eso. Psych.*, I, p. 25). "The sixth Ray of Devotion embodies the principle of recognition. By this I mean the capacity to see the ideal reality lying behind the form; this implies a one-pointed application of desire and of intelligence in order to produce an expression of that sensed idea. It is responsible for much of the formulation of the ideas which have led man on, and for much of the emphasis on the appearance which has veiled and hidden those ideals. It is on this ray primarily — as it cycles in and out of manifestation — that the work of distinguishing between appearance and quality is carried forward, and this work has its field of activity upon the astral plane. The complexity of this subject and the acuteness of the feeling evolved become therefore apparent" (*Eso. Psych.*, I, p. 52).

Some of the qualities, characteristics and factors associated with the sixth ray are: capacity to envision Reality, idealism, one-pointed devotion which negatively can lead to fanaticism, loyalty, tenderness, love with an isolating devotion, an ardent desire for the good, reverence, religious instincts, intense personal feeling, impracticality, superstition, unintelligent work on the physical plane, excessive enthusiasm, relentless pursuit, aspiration, mysticism, and sacrifice.

The Seventh Ray of Ceremonial Order or Magic "embodies a curious quality which . . . is the coordinating factor unifying the inner quality and the outer tangible form or appearance. This work goes on primarily on etheric levels and involves physical energy. This is the true magical work" (*Eso. Psych.*, I, p. 52). "The spiritualizing of forms might be regarded as the main work of the seventh ray, and it is this principle of fusion, of coordination and of blending which is active on etheric levels every time a soul comes into incarnation and a child is born on earth" (*Eso. Psych,* I, p. 53).

Some qualities, characteristics and factors associated with the seventh ray are: ritual, ceremonial living, order and organization, rule and precedent, relating spirit and matter, spiritualizing of forms, extreme care in details, formalism, gift of healing, power to enlighten physical plane living, also glamour of astral magic, "narrowness, superficial judgements and self-opinion over-indulged" (*Eso. Psych.*, I, p. 210).